Praise for
Releasing the Rivers Within

"This book will challenge you to let God do more in your life than you thought possible. God has a supernatural life for us waiting to be lived, and Dwight shows us how we can experience it."

—DR. ERWIN W. LUTZER, senior pastor of The Moody Church
  in Chicago

"Nothing exhilarates like God! Thanks for reminding us, Dwight, that we were created for more than religion."

—BETH MOORE, author, speaker, and president of Living Proof
  Ministries

"Few books leave me in tears of hope. This one did. Dwight lives in this world, but his eyes are fixed on the new covenant, in all its wonder and possibilities. When I finished reading, I knew I could settle for nothing less than the life Jesus makes available."

—LARRY CRABB, author, speaker, psychologist, and founder
  of New Way Ministries

"This book encourages, stimulates, and challenges us to become more like Jesus Christ and tells us the 'why, how, and what' to consider in doing so. Practical, understandable, and applicable to a believer's daily life, it points us to a life characterized by 'deep roots, supernatural fruit, and extending branches' by allowing God to work through us."

—JACK A. TURPIN, chairman of Hallmark Energy, LLC.,
  and coauthor of *Beyond the Bottom Line*

"Peace on earth, the angelic birth announcement for Jesus Christ, incites revolution in every heart. A longing for His peace, a thirst for spiritual knowledge, and a desperate desire to control temptations produce deep unrest. With seasoned pastoral compassion, Dwight Edwards steps up alongside his readers with supplies for living above one's personal war zone. This timely biblical strategy for inner composure in the Christian life belongs on every believer's bookshelf."

—HOWARD G. HENDRICKS, distinguished professor and chairman,
Center for Christian Leadership, Dallas Theological Seminary

"Intelligent and accessible, *Releasing the Rivers Within* goes one step further than *Revolution Within* by convincing me that the answer to many of my personal questions and struggles is not a *what* but a *Who*. Dwight—a personal friend and counselor to me—and his writing continue to be two of the sharpest tools used by God to unearth the new man He birthed within me."

—SHAUN GROVES, recording artist

DWIGHT EDWARDS

the EXHILARATION of
UTTER DEPENDENCE on GOD

RELEASING THE RIVERS WITHIN

foreword by MAX LUCADO

WATERBROOK
PRESS

RELEASING THE RIVERS WITHIN
PUBLISHED BY WATERBROOK PRESS
2375 Telstar Drive, Suite 160
Colorado Springs, Colorado 80920
A division of Random House, Inc.

ISBN 1-57856-460-3

Published in association with Yates & Yates, LLP, Attorneys and Counselors, Orange, California.

Library of Congress Cataloging-in-Publication Data
Edwards, Dwight, 1954–
    Releasing the rivers within : the exhilaration of utter dependence on God /
by Dwight Edwards.— 1st ed.
        p. cm.
    ISBN 1-57856-460-3
    1. Christian life. 2. Spiritual life—Christianity. I. Title.
    BV4501.3.E385 2003
    248.4—dc21
                                                                2003011384

Printed in the United States of America
2003—First Edition

10 9 8 7 6 5 4 3 2 1

To Stephen, Jordan, and Brandon—the three finest sons
any father could hope to have. I so admire each of you
and so enjoy watching you develop as men of God.
May your waters run deeply, strongly, and dependently.

Contents

Foreword

If your energy level is always high, attitude perpetually positive, and faith ever forward-facing, don't mess with this book. You don't need it.

If you, like me, however, occasionally see the needle of your joy-gauge bounce against the empty side, Dwight Edwards has a word for you. A good word.

Present within you is a power—a supernatural power. Your decision to follow Christ triggers His deposit of *Himself* within you. Dwight's aim is to teach us to trust and tap into that strength.

He does it so well. If you read his first book, *Revolution Within,* you know what I mean. My wife loves the project so much she's distributed a case-full. I share her sentiments. Dwight reminded me that Christianity, at its core, is blatantly supernatural.

He continues that theme in this book. With careful exposition and practical application, he not only reveals the river, he shows us the best place to step in! Thanks, Dwight, for your faithful work on this essential topic.

And congratulations to you, the reader, on selecting the right book. May you discover the river, His river within you.

—MAX LUCADO

Acknowledgments

There is no way to properly recognize or thank the many, many people who have been part of seeing this message and book come to fruition. But among the many I would especially like to thank are...

First and foremost, my wife, Sandy Edwards. No one pays a higher price for my writing. Thank you so much for your love, encouragement, and patience.

The men who have so deeply impacted my life: Gene Stogner (thanks for being so much more than a coach), Dave Anderson (I'm still building on the foundation you laid), Larry Crabb (words cannot express my thanks for your friendship and influence), Lanier Burns (how I cherish our friendship and the many great talks over the years), and Walt Baker (your love and example have meant so much). None of you will ever know how much I appreciate each of you.

My editor, Thomas Womack: What an incredible joy to be able to work with you.

My friends at WaterBrook Press who have been as much a family as publishers: Don Pape, Laura Barker, and Kirsten Blomquist. Thank you for encouragement and expertise.

Dan Rich, for seeing the importance of this message; Doug Gabbert, for your encouragement along the way; and Sealy Yates, for your wisdom, guidance, and warm heart.

Some of the greatest church staff around. I have been privileged to work with people who have been such a blessing and help to me. Thank you so much Brian and Tristie Fisher, Brad and Susan

Evans, Pat and Jeanne Coyle, Zack Nigliazzo, Don and Mary Campbell, James and Lainie Moore, Rod and Rae Lynn Mitchell. Special thanks to Annie Carpenter for such great help in source documentation.

Very special friends who have meant so much to Sandy and me over the years: Larry and Rachael Crabb, Doy and Nolan Shipman, David and Julia Gardner, Mike and Sara Grage. Your love and input have both strengthened and changed us.

The T-M family: Jack and Sally Turpin, Scott and Carol Turpin, Jeff and Lori Turpin, Mark and Kathy Turpin, Johnny and Sherri Polk. Each of you has been such a blessing to our lives.

Friends who have given such helpful feedback on this material: Tom and Christel Brymer, Harry and Chris Wilson, Becky Segrest, John Manning, Pam Wiley (thank you for your tireless work on the original manuscript), and Dick Davison. Also Darce Maree, Carolyn and Rick Jones, Jeff and Beth Paine, Ed and Linda Cole, Gary and Wendy McCord. Thursday nights were such a blessing in so many ways. Thank you so much.

The Tuesday morning group: Mike Gentry, Chip Howard, Rob Schleider. Thanks guys for your hearts and sharpening influence. Also Mike Russell, Rick Rigsby, and Chris Reynolds, for your help and encouragement.

Finally, the congregation of Grace Bible Church, especially its elders and deacons. How privileged I am to minister among you and how deeply you have blessed both me and my family.

Made for the White Water

A blistering summer sun in the Texas Hill Country made it a great afternoon to be in the cool waters of the Guadalupe River. We had joined several other families in tubing down the river, laughing and splashing one another's rafts as we lazily floated along.

Most of the time we drifted slowly down the waterway. But a few times when the river picked up speed, we found ourselves swiftly carried along in white water—a blessed relief from the snail-like pace we'd been keeping.

I noticed an interesting thing that afternoon. At certain portions of the river, people would get out, carry their rafts along the bank upstream, then get in to ride down these stretches again. Guess which places these were? You got it. The white water. Nobody wanted more of the slow drifting. But several of us, myself included, went back to reexperience the brief rush of losing control and being swept along in the fastest currents. Slow-moving waters offered plenty of relaxed comfort, but excitement and adventure came only where the water was white.

And so it is with life. Especially our Christian lives.

Something within all of us militates against unrelieved sameness, even when it involves our own personal comfort, safety, and security. The depths of our beings cry out (if we'll listen closely) for a cause greater than ourselves, a launching out into uncharted waters, an unbridled assault upon life. We were made to soar, and our hearts can never know the thrill of this God-ordained flight while our wings are clipped, even though what's clipping them may be pleasant and comfortable.

Something within us recoils at John Stott's description of those whose motto is "safety first" and who "are looking for a safe job in which they can feather their nest, secure their future, insure their lives, reduce all risks, and retire on a fat pension...until life becomes soft and padded and all adventure is gone."[1]

"Human nature, if it is healthy, demands excitement," wrote Oswald Chambers. "God never made bloodless stoics; He makes passionate saints."[2]

Perhaps this is one reason for the popularity of fast-paced, action-packed movies. Film critic George Grella attributes the success of James Bond movies to the fact that Bond "lives the dreams of countless drab people."[3] How sad that we so often try to quiet our hearts' cry for adventure and excitement by experiencing it vicariously through others' risk-taking—especially when God has provided for this need in spades.

You and I were made for the white water. Within every believer, without exception, divine waters eagerly press forward to be released into the lives of others as well as into a desperately needy world. The releasing of these waters will be the riskiest and most exciting thing you'll ever do with your life. It's the key to white-water living for every child of God.

Christ has created and redeemed each of us to be His unique and personal waterway, through whom He can cause His living waters to spill forth for the glory of God, the good of others, and the damage of Satan. Apart from Him we're only bone-dry riverbeds, having nothing of eternal consequence to offer anyone. Yet *through Him*—ah, what a difference that makes!—every life has monumental potential for dispensing the living waters of God to the parched souls of men. And as His waters are dynamically released from within, we experience the exhilaration of utter dependence on God and His strong flow through our lives.

VIBRANT REST

That's what this book is all about—an approach to life and ministry that absolutely requires God and says that without Him we don't even need to bother showing up. It's about leaving behind safe, predictable, boring spirituality for the ride of your life. It's a humble attempt to expound the essentials of what I believe Paul meant when he wrote about our serving God "in the newness of the Spirit and not in the oldness of the letter" (Romans 7:6).

This book is about the high adventure of living under the spell and sway of what the Bible calls "the new covenant" (2 Corinthians 3:6). It's about seeking to understand the reasons behind the glad shout that the whole of our existence begins and ends with God, for when the Christian life is properly lived, *all* the glory must go to God because *all* the good comes from God.

In the following chapters we'll examine what this God-infused good is and how it can be released through us for the benefit of others and, most of all, for the glory of God.

It's the vibrant rest of true spirituality.

What do I mean by vibrant rest?

It's another way of expressing what Jesus had in mind: "Come to Me, all you who labor and are heavy laden, and I will give you rest. Take My yoke upon you and learn from Me, for I am gentle and lowly in heart, and you will find rest for your souls. For My yoke is easy and My burden is light" (Matthew 11:28-30).

If you reflect deeply on those words, you can't help being impressed by the offer Jesus makes: Rest from the weight of sin, rest from the burden of guilt, rest from the tyranny of pressured obedience, rest from enslavement to men's approval, rest from trying to measure up to God's perfect standard—all are included here.

This wondrous rest of soul is in no way anemic, sluggish, or uninvolved. In fact, it's just the opposite. It's experienced only as we live in the exhilarating bondage of being inseparably yoked to the risen Christ. It means quietly and confidently abandoning ourselves to the control of God's white-water currents as they carry us forward in the direction He's heading.

Accompanying this flow is a God-energized, Christ-impassioned, spiritually vibrant rest that's intensely active, yet never pressured, frantic, or guilt driven. It's what I believe Jesus meant in John 15 by the word *abide*. It's what Francis Schaeffer aptly described as "active passivity."

Our vibrant rest is the glorious by-product of allowing God's "rivers of living water" to flow out of our innermost being (see John 7:37-39). In the words of Dr. Larry Crabb, it means "releasing what is good"—and the "good" he speaks of is the life of Christ in our souls. As we abide in Him and allow His life to break forth through ours, we experience an energetic peace that defies description but not experience.

In my book *Revolution Within,* I focused on what it means to have rivers of living water dwelling *within* us. In this book I want to deal with what it means to have these rivers flow out *through* us into this broken, sin-sick world. I want to help you see what it looks like to have the life of God within us transported to the believers and unbelievers around us.

RADICAL, NAKED DEPENDENCE

Why is this so important? Why bother to put out another book on Christian living and ministry when so many helpful ones are on the market already?

I find myself compelled to write because of two central truths I want to emphasize. You'll find these same truths in other books, but candidly, such books are too few and were mainly written for previous generations.

My prayer is that the Spirit of God will be pleased to use this work to reawaken believers to these two core realities.

One of those realities is this: *The kind of Christian living and ministry that exerts greatest influence for God is always based upon a Who rather than a what.* The list of things promised in our day as keys to godly living and effective ministry keeps growing—spiritual disciplines, biblical knowledge, being personally discipled, fasting, ministry involvement, significant fellowship, power encounters, personal accountability, leadership principles. All these are only "whats"—and while they have their place, they're ineffective on their own.

This is why, after Paul's confession of his wretchedness in battling sin in Romans 7, his subsequent question is so important: "Who will deliver me from this body of death?" (Romans 7:24). He doesn't ask *what* will deliver him but *Who*. A what can never deliver us from sin; only a Who can do that.

Only a Who can flow through us to bring forth eternally significant ministry, as Paul knew: "I will not venture to speak of anything except *what Christ has accomplished through me*...by what I have said and done" (Romans 15:18, NIV). Paul saw the entire success of his ministry as a result of one factor alone: Christ, Christ, Christ! Jesus wore Paul as His personal suit of clothes; through Paul's yielded body, Jesus could walk, talk, and—most of all—love.

Paul knew what it was to live in the white water of Christ's life rushing though him. This can be our experience, too. It is, in fact, our sole hope for having genuinely supernatural and lasting impact on others: Christ within us being allowed to relive His life through us.

Reading those words, you probably agree with me already. Yet how easy it is for us to subtly move away from radical, naked dependence upon our indwelling Who and instead to depend, at least in part, on the many good whats available to us.

Clearly there's a place in our lives for the whats. How then do we properly utilize them without depending upon them? What does it look like for our life and ministry to be carried out in such a way that the scorch marks of the supernatural are unmistakably visible? These are some of the questions we'll explore throughout this book.

A STARTLING OUTBREAK OF GOD

Here's the second core reality I want to emphasize: *Handiwork worthy of the name of God can be produced only by God.*

We exist on this planet for one central, overriding purpose—God's glory. What is His glory? Although there's no way through the frail medium of human language to adequately describe or define it, I like to think of God's glory as His stunning, surprising spectacularness. It's His incessant off-the-chartness. On a scale of one to ten, every one of His attributes is a twenty and beyond.

God's glory isn't surprising to Him in the least, but to us it radiates a grandeur and splendor that rivets our attention, ravishes our affections, and draws us into a wide-eyed, breathless wonder experienced nowhere else.

What then does it mean to glorify God?

It means to be supremely satisfied in Him over all competitors. It means living a life that flaunts His excellencies before a watching world.

And it means our lives will pack an element of supernatural surprise. God can't be glorified in lives that fail to go beyond what religious flesh can pull off on its own. Our existence must demonstrate more than predictable morality and run-of-the-mill kindness; our lives must disclose a visible, startling outbreak of God, a breathtaking display of divine artisanship.

Think of the Christians in the church's earliest centuries. While far from being perfect, they nonetheless rocked the Roman world back on its heels with the gospel of Christ. No generation of believers since has had as great an influence for Christ in a shorter amount of time than those early saints. What was their secret?

Several things led to the incredible impact of the first Christians. One was their bold proclamation of the Word. Another was their unshakable belief that Jesus alone was Lord. And according to the observations of pagan governors and philosophers of the time, three qualities in particular caught the attention of those around them:

These believers had *a joy that couldn't be explained.* Unbelievers recognized in them a deep and abiding sense of something even greater than happiness. It was a radiant joy that made no sense, given their difficult circumstances.

They also displayed *a peace that couldn't be sabotaged.* Routinely, these Christians would submit to cruel death with a calm serenity that defied understanding.

Above all, they demonstrated *a love that couldn't be imitated.* Their love for one another left observers scratching their heads.

How badly we need these same three qualities in our day! What will impact our world most powerfully is not telling people how wrong they are, but once again exposing them to a joy that can't be explained, a peace that can't be sabotaged, and a love that can't be imitated.

GOD DOES THE FLAUNTING

But there's a major problem with all this. We can't do it! It's like asking a one-year-old to play Mozart or a physically handicapped person to run in the Olympics. This degree of love and joy and peace is too far beyond our natural ability; if that's what it takes to glorify God, we may as well close up shop and go home.

Fortunately, God has the answer to our dilemma.

You may have noticed that each of these three—love, joy, peace— are included in "the fruit of the Spirit" (Galatians 5:22-23). These are characteristics God's Spirit produces, not what we produce ourselves. We can't flaunt the excellencies of God before a watching world unless God does the flaunting!

This is why Paul prayed that we might be "filled with the fruits of righteousness which are *by* Jesus Christ, to the glory and praise of God" (Philippians 1:11). In large measure, that verse is what this book is all about—bringing forth Christ-produced fruit so we can live a God-spotlighted life. It's about how to become a river of God, so the currents of Christ's indwelling life can flow through us mightily and surprisingly, to the glory of the Father and the good of others.

The result? A white-water life coupled with a vibrant rest.

Come, my friend; let me invite you to come along on the same journey that I, very imperfectly, am taking myself.

Trust me—it will be the ride of your life.

His River Runs Through

If you believe in Jesus, you will find
that God has nourished in you
mighty torrents of blessing for others.
Oswald Chambers

During the early 1920s, Ira and Ann Yates were eking out a sparse living on the ranch they owned in west Texas. Their land was barren and parched by drought. Requiring government subsidy just to get by, they despaired of making ends meet, let alone getting ahead.

That is, until October 28, 1926. That evening, a drilling company struck oil on their property for the first time. Soon the well was producing more than sixty thousand barrels per day.

This was dwarfed a few weeks later by the discovery of another well that would eventually produce over two hundred thousand barrels per day. Many additional wells were later drilled, and today this land, known as Yates Field, has reserves estimated at more than one billion barrels, the largest of any oil field in the United States other than Prudhoe Bay in Alaska. In the meantime, the Yates family has received hundreds of millions of dollars and has donated millions to various causes.

I wonder how many years the Yates family merely existed on the land, never dreaming that less than a thousand feet beneath them lay unimaginable treasure, that within their grasp lay the resources not only to meet their own needs and more, but to enable them to outlandishly bless others?

What a difference knowing your resources can make!

If you know Jesus, then *you* are like Yates Field. Buried within you and every believer are outlandish and inexhaustible resources, implanted and sustained by God alone, capable of abundantly meeting our deepest needs and mightily blessing those around us. Yet, like the Yates family, many of us aren't even aware of our indwelling treasure—or at least we fail to comprehend its full extent. Far too often we're living like Ira and Ann in the early years, eking out a spiritual existence and trying our best not to succumb to powerful temptations that seem so overwhelming. "Vibrant rest" isn't exactly the phrase we would use to describe our walk with God. Our souls are parched, our spirits weary, and the thought of becoming a significant blessing to others' lives feels like an intolerably heavy "should."

There seems to be so little of God for our own souls; how could we possibly impart Him to others? What often feels most real to us is that we live on a spiritual bread line, just making it from one quiet time to another, one worship service to the next. Whatever Jesus meant by the abundant life, it must be intended for other believers. We'd like for things to be different, but we feel mired in the daily routines of life, which draw so much out of us while depositing so little within.

What cause do we have for believing that things really could be different? That there really are dynamic, untapped resources residing within each of us?

What do these resources look like, how can we get to them, and most of all, how do we appropriate their abundance?

Let me take you back to a day two thousand years ago when Jesus spoke to these very issues. His words are recorded in my favorite passage in all of God's Word concerning the radical and dynamic outflow of New Covenant living:

On the last day, that great day of the feast, Jesus stood and cried
out, saying, "If anyone thirsts, let him come to Me and drink. He
who believes in Me, as the Scripture has said, out of his heart will
flow rivers [literally, floods or torrents] of living water." But this
He spoke concerning the Spirit, whom those believing in Him
would receive; for the Holy Spirit was not yet given, because Jesus
was not yet glorified. (John 7:37-39)

Let those words of Jesus sink deeply into your heart. "He who believes
in Me...out of his heart will flow torrents of living water." Take a moment
to prayerfully ponder them, then come back to the next paragraph.

Beginning with this promise of our Lord, let's explore four truths, four
central arteries that carry the lifeblood of a New Covenant approach to life
and ministry.

TORRENTS OF LIVING WATERS

The first truth: *You're permanently inflooded with divine abundance.* The
word in John 7:38 for "rivers" is frequently translated as "floods" (as in
Matthew 7:25,27 and Revelation 12:15-16); "torrents" is another possible
rendering of the Greek. You, my friend, are home to a spiritual deluge,
with torrents of divine waters pressing forward for release from deep
within. Your cup isn't just full; it's running over! (see Psalm 23:5).

What are these rivers of living waters? Scripture clearly answers: "This
He spoke concerning *the Spirit*" (John 7:39). The precious Holy Spirit, in
all His abundance and with all His activities, is the One being pictured as
rivers of living water. Only through the Holy Spirit will the living, breathing, pulsating presence of God take up residence in the deep corridors of
our heart. Only through the Spirit can we quench the raging thirst God
has placed in our souls and go on to supernaturally bless others' lives.

The starting place for this experience is to understand well the various provisions and privileges believers receive when the Holy Spirit enters their life at conversion. Because of the New Covenant we become permanent recipients of a new purity, a new identity, a new disposition, and a new power. In Peter's words, we become "partakers of the divine nature" and are granted "all things that pertain to life and godliness" (2 Peter 1:3-4). Everything we need to satisfy our yearning hearts and radiate godliness into our daily lives is supplied through the Holy Spirit, the river of God coursing through our souls.

How desperately we need to be reminded of this reality! So often we find ourselves tottering under the weight of family pressures, work deadlines, personal responsibilities, fleshly temptations, spiritual duties, and more. Our heart despairs of ever having what it takes to meet the constant demands coming our way. Subtly, we begin to believe life is found in somehow alleviating these outside pressures. "If only I didn't have to..." "If only I could get rid of..." "If only there weren't so much..." These are our supposed stepping stones to the happiness that eludes us.

Jesus provides another path to life. It's not the alleviation of outside pressures and responsibilities, but the appropriation of indwelling rivers. "You give them drink from the river of Your pleasures. For with You is the fountain of life; in Your light we see light" (Psalm 36:8-9). As always, God's answer to our deepest needs is simply Himself. And His provision for impacting others through us is likewise simply Himself.

RELEASING GOD'S RESTLESSNESS

The second lifeblood truth of the New Covenant is this: *You're permanently indwelt by an "on the move" God.* The Spirit of God within us is clearly on the move, on the "flow" out of our hearts, as Jesus said in John 7:38. In fact, the phrase *living waters* was synonymous in those days with "running water." Everything in this passage speaks of movement, of a forward urging that refuses to stop or stagnate.

This ought not surprise us, as the Holy Spirit is never seen as passive or static in the Scriptures. He's described as "the seven Spirits of God sent out into all the earth" (Revelation 5:6). He's "a fountain of water springing up into everlasting life" (John 4:14). The Spirit of God within the new heart of the believer is continually spouting upward toward heaven for communion with and worship of the Father. Whether or not you feel it at the moment, God's Spirit within you is on the move in an upward direction toward the Father through the Son.

Our pursuit of God is ultimately a gifted pursuit, as A. W. Tozer points out: "We pursue God because, and only because, He has first put an urge within us that spurs us to that pursuit."[1] It requires God within us to pursue God above us. Fortunately, this is something He specializes in.

Yes, the Spirit of God within us not only springs upward but also flows outward, incessantly. That puts into proper perspective where our passion for God and ministry are ultimately derived. It's not a self-generated disciplining of our will, but a full cooperation with the tug of the Holy Spirit who wants to carry us away in the divine currents of His flow. Within every believer stirs a supernaturally inbred restlessness that is wholly the result of being indwelt by the Holy Spirit. We can grieve the Spirit, quench the Spirit, resist the Spirit, or generally neglect the Spirit, but we can never shake free from His Person or lay to rest His passion. He remains on the move, whether we come along for the ride or not.

This truth of "God on the move" within us runs contrary to how so many believers view their Christian experience. They believe that the responsibility for spiritual passion rests solely on their own shoulders: If they could just pray more, be more consistent in devotions, deal more decisively with secret sins, surrender more fully, and be more involved in ministry and sharing their faith…then surely they would experience greater zeal for the Lord. They believe their own obedience is what will stir the waters of God's movement in their souls. It all depends on them—on how well they respond to God's calling on their lives.

But maybe, just maybe, this is all backward. If I understand the New Covenant correctly, the waters of God's movement in our hearts are already pressing forward, whether we're obedient or not.

When we trusted Christ for salvation, we received "an inward fervency and light," as Martin Luther termed it; by that inward light "we are changed and become new creatures" and "we also receive a new judgment, a new feeling, and a new moving"; and the Holy Spirit brings forth within us what Luther called "spiritual motions."[2]

When we step forward in godly responsiveness, it's because the Father is invigorating the powerful resources that already lie within us. We don't do godly acts in order to "get things moving"; we do them *because* things are already moving.

True obedience, therefore, means the joy of tangibly releasing God's restlessness in our souls, the same restlessness of God that inhabits every believer. This is the foundational energy for all true movement, upward or outward, in the Christian life.

REDEEMED TO MAKE A DIFFERENCE

This is the third lifeblood truth of the New Covenant: *You were created to make a supernatural and eternal difference in this world.* God has no insignificant saints or unimportant believers in His kingdom. In the words of Francis Schaeffer, there are no "little people" in God's family. Every believer has a vital part to play in time and eternity—not because of who we are, but because of who God is within us.

Notice the condition for becoming a river of spiritual blessing to those around us. Jesus didn't say, "He who believes in Me and has formal theological training" or "He who believes in Me and has the gift of evangelism or teaching" or "He who believes in Me and is a gifted leader." The invitation to being mightily used by God is given to but one group—"whosoever." Whosoever will come to Jesus, whosoever will drink deeply of Him in an ongoing manner, whosoever will open the floodgates of their lives in risking, daring faith—they and they alone will taste the clean and deep joy of seeing their waters spill over into others' lives. Only it won't be their waters, but the river of God through them. "If you believe in Jesus," Oswald Chambers says, "you will find that God has nourished in you mighty torrents of blessing for others."[3]

On this truth, how I wish I had time to walk you through the halls of the Bible and of church and missions history! How I would love to point out to you the portraits of countless men and women through the ages who had nothing going for them but God. Moses, Gideon, David, Moody, Carey, Taylor, Booth, and innumerable others bear undeniable witness to the reality that all true success is divinely gifted and supernaturally imparted success. "Your fruit is found in Me" (Hosea 14:8) is the bedrock for all genuinely spiritual ministry.

Christ purposefully used "uneducated and untrained men" (Acts 4:13) to lay the foundation of the church. The continuation of the church and the advance of the gospel have come primarily not through the wise, mighty, or noble, but through the foolish, weak, and base (see 1 Corinthians 1:26-29). When one has little or nothing to fall back on naturally, then God ceases to be a good option. He becomes a desperate necessity, just like the air we breathe.

You were redeemed to make a difference—an everlasting difference. After saving you through the blood of His only Son and taking up permanent residence in your soul through His Spirit, God didn't then strand you here on earth with no purposes but your own till He takes you home. Right now, right here—right where you live, where you work, where you worship, where you recreate, where you shop, where your kids go to school, where you take your car for repairs, where you get your hair cut—

you're His flesh-and-blood advertising agency, a human riverbank through whom His streams can cascade forth.

You and I have the potential to make an eternal difference in eternal souls for the greatest cause on earth—the eternal glory of God. Yet this everlasting difference can occur only as we forsake the subtle temptation to influence others through the strength of our personality or gifting or intellect, and instead rely exclusively on the gifted strength, love, and wisdom of the indwelling river of God. "To cling to my natural virtues," notes Oswald Chambers, "is quite sufficient to obscure the work of God in me."[4] Only the Spirit flowing through us can make a lasting, God-honoring difference in those around us.

This, my friend, is Christ's grand calling on your life regardless of who you are, where you've been, what you've done, or what's been done to you. God has made you a difference-maker, allowing you the high privilege and opportunity to transport His living water to other thirsting souls.

THE SOURCE OF SOUL SATISFACTION

The fourth New Covenant truth states: *You'll never be fully satisfied until the floodgates of your life are opened wide.*

For years I struggled with the words of Jesus in John 7:37-38. They just didn't appear to be true. If all believers are promised rivers of living water flowing out of them, then where's all that water? When you think about all that's promised and then look out on the body of Christ today, you can't help but wonder why so much is missing.

I believe the ultimate answer is this: Christ promised that the waters were "on the flow" internally ("out of his heart"), but He didn't guarantee they would make their way to the outside. For this to happen, the floodgates of our lives must be opened. And the wider they're open, the fuller the flow and the deeper the joy.

One of the many things we receive at our conversion is a divinely implanted sense of discontent with trivial living. Something deep down in every believer militates against living an ordinary, comfortable, risk-free existence.

Too many of us live in what Oswald Sanders called "a fur lined rut." Though life may be comfortable and safe on the outside, we can't escape the dissatisfaction haunting us on the inside. The Spirit within us is an eternal Spirit and refuses to be pacified by temporal, finite pursuits.

While our lives will always require involvement with temporal things and issues, they can never find true contentment in these things. God has "put eternity" in our hearts (Ecclesiastes 3:11), and this God-shaped vacuum can be filled only by a God-sized purpose.

That's why Isaiah asks, "Why do you spend money for what is not bread, and your wages for what does not satisfy? Listen carefully to Me, and eat what is good, and let your soul delight itself in abundance" (Isaiah 55:2).

When I was in college, a group of us held a worship service in a nursing home. In our group was a girl named Kika, who had become a Christian a few months before. She came from one of the wealthiest families in Switzerland, had attended the finest of schools, and had experienced just about everything this world has to offer.

Kika jumped enthusiastically into our ministry work that day and helped to persuade some of the more reclusive nursing home residents to come out of their rooms and attend our service. She loved well the people who were there.

When the service was over and most of the people had gone back to their rooms, I saw her back in the corner crying. I went over to see what was wrong. "Kika," I asked, "what's the matter? What went wrong?"

Through her tears she looked up at me and said, "Dwight, I've never been so happy in all my life. I never knew such joy existed."

Having tasted so much of what the world prescribes for happiness, she now had found a depth of joy that comes only through opening wide the floodgates of our life for God's living water to pass through. She had discovered the great paradox of soul satisfaction:

> If you extend your soul to the hungry
> And satisfy the afflicted soul,
> Then your light shall dawn in the darkness,
> And your darkness shall be as the noonday.
> The LORD will guide you continually,
> And satisfy your soul in drought,
> And strengthen your bones;
> You shall be like a watered garden,
> And like a spring of water, whose waters do not fail.
>   (Isaiah 58:10-11)

ALWAYS MORE THAN ENOUGH

As I write this, I realize that for far too long I've been putting off meeting with another believer who I know has some things against me. I've had a number of rationalizations for putting this off, none of which the Holy Spirit has found convincing! I've come to realize that one of my main obstacles has been a sense of being overwhelmed by the potential heaviness of the encounter, the weight of possible difficulties attached to it. Therefore, I've subtly believed the lie that life is found (at least in part) by not having this meeting, or at least postponing it as long as possible.

What helps me most to escape such erroneous thinking is to focus on Christ within—His unshakable love, His perfect wisdom, His enabling power. My only hope for moving into this uncomfortable situation is relying on the rivers He has placed within to carry me along in their currents of love, wisdom, and power.

Since I wrote the preceding paragraph, God has enabled me to finally reach out and contact the brother I mentioned. I did it with fear and trepidation, but also in desperate dependence upon something deeper than my anxieties—the rivers of living water supernaturally flowing within. This alone was able to override the pull of my flesh.

In case you're wondering how it went, the answer is, even worse than expected. I'm still hurt by this man's response and feel misunderstood. But beneath all this is the clean satisfaction of having allowed God to flow through me, regardless of the outcome. Truly experiencing the vibrant rest of God has nothing to do with changing circumstances on the outside; it has everything to do with the Holy Spirit flowing on the inside.

Because of the divine abundance inflooding our souls, there's an important truth for us to remember: To enable us to carry out His will, God is always ready to give us *more than enough* of Himself. "Now to Him who is able to do exceedingly abundantly above all that we ask or think, according to the power that works in us" (Ephesians 3:20). God's economy in our souls is always one of surplus. He's able to provide not just the necessary strength we need to make it through this trial, but more than we can use. He can give us more than enough love to reach out to a disagreeable person, and more than enough patience for every difficult relationship.

"God will load your world with flowers," Max Lucado writes in *A Love Worth Giving*. "He hand-delivers a bouquet to your door every day. Open it! Take it! Then when rejections come, you won't find yourself short-petaled."[5]

When Jesus made His promise in John 7 about the never-ending flow of living waters, He prefaced it with the words, "As the Scripture has said…" No single Old Testament passage fully matches the statement Jesus made, but one that may well have been in His thinking richly describes "the river of God" as a stream of amazing abundance. The passage is Ezekiel 47:1-12, and I urge you now to look up this portion of God's Word and take a moment to prayerfully and worshipfully meditate upon it.

We see in this passage that wherever the waters of this "river of God" flow, they bring life (47:9), healing (47:8-9,12), and fruitfulness (47:12). And we especially get a strong description of the abundance of these waters.

As an angelic guide led the prophet Ezekiel out into the river, Ezekiel first encountered water that was ankle deep, then knee deep, then waist deep. Finally, "it was a river that I could not cross; for the water was too deep, water in which one must swim, a river that could not be crossed" (47:3-5).

What a fitting portrait of the Holy Spirit within the believer!

There's more Spirit available to us than we can ever use. We aren't ankle-deep, knee-deep, or even waist-deep saints. We're in over our heads! The Spirit within us is too deep ever to touch bottom and too wide to ever be crossed in a lifetime of appropriating.

These lines from Frederick W. Faber capture this well:

> Thou art a Sea without a shore,
> awesome, immense Thou art;
> a Sea which can contract itself,
> within my tiny heart.[6]

Obviously, there are many times it doesn't feel like this abundant river is flowing within. Some days we'd be content just to be toe-deep Christians. The idea of torrents of living waters within us seems so implausible; we'd be glad just to feel some trickles! Yet we must be careful not to dismiss or downplay the extravagance of what God's Word offers simply because the level of our present experience hasn't scaled the heights of our Lord's offer.

Martyn Lloyd-Jones warned of the danger of "being satisfied with something very much less than what's offered in the Scripture, and the danger of interpreting Scripture by our experiences and reducing its teaching to the level of what we know and experience."[7] When our experience doesn't match what Scripture appears to offer, the worst thing we can do is interpret the passage in such a way as to bring it down to the level of our experience, thereby subtly vindicating ourselves. Instead, we should ask God to raise our experience to the level of the passage, saving us from downsizing the magnitude of the offer He makes.

A question posed by the angelic guide to Ezekiel is the one we need to start with as well: "Son of man, have you seen this?" (Ezekiel 47:6). God was telling Ezekiel, "Have your eyes feasted upon the sight before you and have your memory banks stored it all away? For the day is coming when all this will not seem very real to you."

Likewise, the starting point for us is never what feels or seems most real, but what *is* most real according to the divine plan and provisions of God. And what *is* most real is that we're permanently inflooded with a divine abundance flowing continuously to more than meet our needs and to water the depths of our thirsty souls. Whether or not it seems or feels like it, we're permanently "blessed…with *every spiritual blessing* in the heavenly places in Christ" (Ephesians 1:3).

Child of God, have you seen this?

A PERPETUAL FORWARD FLOW

God has not only inflooded our souls with divine waters, He has also stirred those waters into a perpetual forward flow. The life of Christ relentlessly pushes forward for expression within every believer.

To resist or ignore this forward flow is to invite a spiritual stagnation like the Dead Sea, instead of the freshness of the Sea of Galilee. Bruce Barton tellingly describes these two bodies of water in Palestine:

> There are two seas in the land of Palestine. One is fresh and fish are
> in it. Splashes of green adorn its banks. Trees spread their branches
> over it and stretch out their thirsty roots to sip of its healing waters.

The River Jordan makes this sea with sparkling water from Mount Hermon. Men build their houses near it, birds build their nests by it, and every kind of life is happier because it is there.

The Jordan River flows 60 miles south into another sea. Here there is no splash of fish, no fluttering leaf, no song of birds, no children's laughter. Travelers choose another route unless on business. The air hangs heavy above its waters, which neither man, nor beast, nor fowl will drink.

What makes for this mighty difference in these neighbor seas? Not the Jordan River—it empties the same good water into both. Not the soil in which they lie, nor the country around it.

This is the difference: The Sea of Galilee receives, but does not keep the Jordan. For every drop that flows into it, another flows out. The other sea is shrewd, hoarding its income jealously. It will not be tempted into any generous impulse. Every drop it gets, it keeps.

The Sea of Galilee gives and lives. The other sea gives nothing...it is called the Dead Sea.[8]

What will it take for our lives to experience the vitality, freshness, divine usefulness, adventure, and vibrant rest we all long for and which are the birthright of every child of God? In the next chapter we'll begin exploring those very issues.

Heavenly Connoisseurs

It is a Christian duty, as you know,
for everyone to be as happy as he can.
C. S. Lewis

George Müller was one of the greatest examples of a man becoming a river of God to his generation. During a lifetime of service to the Lord that spanned most of the nineteenth century, he helped build five large orphanages housing some ten thousand orphans, of whom approximately one-third came to know Christ. He received and gave away some seven and a half million dollars to support hundreds of missionaries. He also was involved in Christian publishing and the founding of many educational and religious institutions. From age seventy to eighty-four he traveled more than two hundred thousand miles in forty-two different countries, preaching the gospel to more than three million people.

What was the secret to his widespread and powerful influence for the gospel? His own journal gives us the answer.

While I was staying at Nailsworth, it pleased the Lord to teach me a truth, irrespective of human instrumentality, as far as I know, the benefit of which I have not lost, though now, while preparing the eighth edition for the press, more than forty years have since passed away. The point is this: I saw more clearly than ever, that the first great and primary business to which I ought attend every day was, *to have my soul happy in the Lord.* The first thing to be concerned about was not, how much I might serve the Lord, how I might glorify the Lord; but how I might get my soul into a happy state, and how my inner man may be nourished.[1] (emphasis mine)

This great man of God understood a critical truth spoken by our Lord and experienced by multitudes of fragrant saints throughout history: The prerequisite for flowing freely is drinking deeply. Those involved in heavenly service must first be heavenly connoisseurs, glad and satisfied tasters of heaven's finest cuisine.

Müller also recognized another revolutionary, life-transforming reality: God is someone to be passionately and immensely enjoyed, not merely dutifully served. In fact, He can't be properly served apart from being deeply enjoyed. Holiness and happiness are not mutually exclusive; grim-faced spirituality, sacrificial as it may be, is actually a betrayal of the "blessed [literally, 'happy'] God" (1 Timothy 1:11) whom we serve.

UNBRIDLED ENJOYMENT OF GOD

One of the greatest discoveries of my life was coming to understand that God's desire and design for each of us is to be happily holy and holily happy.

But is that really true? What about all the verses instructing us to deny ourselves and give up our life for Christ and the gospel's sake? Those are nonnegotiable commands of our Lord, and I have no desire to downgrade their importance in our lives. I would simply add this thought: Nowhere in Scripture is self-denial seen as an end in itself, but always a means to a greater end.

For the believer, that greater end is not becoming a dour, rigidly committed disciple of Christ. It's becoming a God-satiated, Christ-intoxicated,

Spirit-empowered worshiper and servant of the Most High God. The reason Paul counted "all things loss" was not to prove something to himself or to God. It was because he had to give up his fleshly trinkets to have room to take hold of the greatest prize of all—"that I may know Him" (Philippians 3:8-11). Genuine, Spirit-induced denial of self always leads to a greater treasure than smug, congratulating of self on being willing to pay the price of true discipleship. It always leads to *Him*.

I'm told that in the Caribbean they catch monkeys by drilling a hole through a coconut and placing peanuts inside. The hole is just large enough for the monkey to get his hand through, but too small to get it out unless he lets go of the peanuts. The coconut is then tied to a tree. The unsuspecting monkey comes along and slips his hand into the coconut to take hold of the peanuts. Because he's so determined to hold on to them, he ultimately forfeits his freedom.

Don't we often do the very same thing? We hold tenaciously to this world's peanuts—sex, alcohol, ambition, hobbies, cars, work, approval of others, money, religious respectability—because sin has duped us into believing life can be found in earthly trinkets. But the quality of life we yearn for and were made for can be found only in a life of unrestrained feasting upon the Bread of Life. There's no greater freedom or exhilaration than this. But as long as we settle for the peanuts of earth, this Bread of Heaven will never have the opportunity to deeply satisfy our divinely implanted taste buds. God calls us to give up the peanuts so we'll have room enough in our mouths for the best there is: Himself.

Yes, we're called to an ongoing life of denying that part of us ("the flesh") that looks for comfort, prestige, security, and pleasure, regardless of the will of God. But why are we to deny this? Because in pursuing those things we leave in the dust the highest good God has for us. Worst of all, we proclaim to the world that our God can't complete the job of meeting the deepest needs of our soul.

Denial of self, in its truly biblical form, will always lead to a godly indulging of self in which self-denial loses its sting and arrogance. We give up the peanuts so we can dine on filet mignon.

Samuel Rutherford pictured this beautifully as the "white side" of the cross. "He who looks at the white side of Christ's cross, and takes it up handsomely, will find it just such a burden as wings are to a bird."[2] The cross will always seem to have its dark side—the calling upon us to deny ourselves, pick up our cross, and follow in the steps of the crucified Christ. This calling must not be minimized. But just as real is the cross's white side, the untainted delight and deep satisfaction of fresh communion with God.

Going hand in hand with our unbridled enjoyment of God is His unrivaled supremacy in Himself, as Jonathan Edwards declares:

> God's respect to the creature's good, and his respect to himself, is
> not a divided respect; but both are united in one, as the happiness
> of the creature aimed at is happiness in union with himself.[3]

"Delight yourself also in the LORD," David tells us, "and He shall give you the desires of your heart" (Psalm 37:4).

This, then, is the foundation for becoming a river of God in our generation. It's the glad and well-watered soul in Christ Jesus flowing freely and purposefully into others' lives.

It won't be a sorrow-free existence; our Lord Himself was "a Man of sorrows and acquainted with grief" (Isaiah 53:3). The main point of our lives, however, will not be suffering and pain, but the divinely enabled fulfilling of our Father's will, just as it was for Jesus. And for this to happen, there must be a spilling forth of the very life of God Himself.

The foundation for this spilling-forth life is found not in activity but in appropriation. Jesus was saying, in effect, in John 7:37, "If anyone thirsts, let him continually come to Me and drink again and again." Here's the prerequisite for rivers of living waters making their way out of our lives: We can't give away what we haven't first received, and God's calling on His people is not primarily to flow freely but to drink deeply.

AN UNQUENCHABLE THIRST

Before we explore our calling to drink deeply, we must begin with the precursor to that call—thirst. "If anyone thirsts" is the description of those Christ is inviting to come. What does He mean?

Throughout Scripture, physical thirst is a metaphor for the spiritual thirst we all have. "O God, You are my God; early will I seek You; my soul thirsts for You; my flesh longs for You in a dry and thirsty land where there is no water" (Psalm 63:1; see also Isaiah 55:1; Revelation 22:17). In his classic work *The Life of God in the Soul of Man,* Henry Scougal concludes, "The soul of man has in it a raging and inextinguishable thirst."[4]

The reason we're so desperately thirsty is that God made us that way. We're born into this world with a divinely implanted thirst, an unshakable parchedness that ultimately can be slaked only in Christ.

God never condemns us in Scripture for our thirst; instead, He pleads with us to drink heartily from the right waters—Himself. Then we'll thank Him for "the river of Your pleasures" and freely offer our praise: "For with You is the fountain of life" (Psalm 36:8-9). Wholeheartedly we'll join with Augustine and confess, "Thou hast made us for Thyself, and our hearts are restless until they find their rest in Thee."

Deeply recognized thirst is the beginning of our movement toward Christ—the shameless embracing of our fiery, upward yearning for divine communion and intimacy.

But what happens if thirst doesn't seem to be there? I would argue from the Scriptures that it's always there, but not necessarily always recognized. We can't eradicate our thirst, but we can divert it or try to deny it.

Do You Recognize Your Thirst?

There are basically three kinds of people in the world.

First are those who are thirsty and realize it. This is true of both believers and unbelievers. In fact, non-Christians often seem more acutely aware of this inward thirst than Christians. So many secular songs and even movies are reflective of the deep human cravings of the soul for love, significance, purpose, and fulfillment. These people may not know what to do with their thirst, but they know for sure it's there.

Asked in an interview if he was at peace with himself, actor Nick Nolte responded,

> There's one thing that's still inside, and that's kind of a yearning. What that yearning is I'm not totally sure. But whatever it is, it can't quite get quenched. I think it's a need, a seeking of completeness. I think that's one quality of life that's common to all of us.

God has made us thirsty, then rigged life so that this thirst can't be fully satisfied outside of Him. "Man's unhappiness," nineteenth-century essayist Thomas Carlyle observed, "comes of his greatness; it is because there is an infinite in him which with all his cunning he cannot quite bury under the finite."

Second, there are people who are thirsty but try to pretend they're not. These individuals essentially are following the path of Buddhism in striving for nirvana, the state of tranquility and contentment that comes from having one's desires extinguished. One is satisfied not because longings have been met, but because longings have been annihilated.

It's like the plaque I once saw picturing a dog lying on the ground with a blank stare. Underneath were the words, "Blessed are those who desire nothing; they shall never be disappointed."

Unfortunately, what's often called contentment among Christians is really little more than sanctified Buddhism. To be concerned for our own pleasure is viewed as carnal, and godly contentment is defined as the ability to go through life without worrying whether our needs are being met.

C. S. Lewis addresses this issue in strong words:

> If there lurks in most modern minds the notion that to desire our own good and earnestly to hope for the enjoyment of it is a bad thing, I submit that this notion has crept in from Kant and the Stoics and is no part of the Christian faith. Indeed, if we consider the unblushing promises of reward and the staggering nature of the rewards promised in the Gospels, it would seem that Our Lord finds our desires not too strong, but too weak. We are half-hearted creatures, fooling about with drink and sex and ambition when infinite joy is offered us, like an ignorant child who wants to go on making mud pies in a slum because he cannot imagine what is meant by the offer of a holiday at the sea. We are far too easily pleased.[5]

True contentment is not pretending that the raging thirst within us is a ghost; it's taking our real thirst with all its passionate neediness and diving headlong into the river of God to drink. "The whole man is to drink joy from the fountain of joy," Lewis also said. And God says, "Open your mouth wide, and I will fill it" (Psalm 81:10).

The third kind of people are those who are thirsty but try to quench their thirst at counterfeit watering holes. This is what the Lord is addressing through the prophet Jeremiah: "For My people have committed two evils: they have forsaken Me, the fountain of living waters, and hewn themselves cisterns—broken cisterns that can hold no water" (Jeremiah 2:13). God doesn't rebuke His people here for being thirsty but only for trying to slake their thirst at stagnant, muddy watering holes.

What a vivid picture this passage gives! God is likened to an ever-flowing fountain of crystal-clear, deeply refreshing waters. No water can quench thirst like God's can.

"God is so vastly wonderful," wrote A. W. Tozer, "so utterly and completely delightful, that He can, without anything other than Himself, meet and overflow the deepest demands of our total nature, mysterious and deep as that nature is."[6] For this reason we can sing to Him as they did in the Psalms, "All my springs are in You" (87:7).

Yet sin has introduced the insane belief that the raging thirst in man can be satisfied by broken cisterns—plastered holes in the ground filled with stagnant water. Illicit sex, drug abuse, materialism, work, ego gratification, and religious activities are just a few of the cisterns we turn to in order to find the soul satisfaction and quality of life we're too afraid to trust God for.

It's like having access to the clear, cold, refreshing water of a stream in the Colorado Rockies and choosing instead to drink from the muddy Rio Grande in Texas. It's not just wrong, it's insane! That's why John Piper defines sin as "the suicidal abandonment of joy."[7]

God says, "Therefore with joy you will draw water from the wells of salvation" (Isaiah 12:3). We assassinate the deep-seated joy God has for each of us when we seek to draw life from the empty and broken cisterns this world so readily offers.

Drinking Deeply from God's Fountain

There's something better than stiff-arming our thirst or being seduced into trying to quench it at the wrong waters. Christ gives a twofold calling for satisfying this burning longing placed in our souls: We're to come to Him, and we're to drink.

"Come to *Me*," Jesus said—not "to My church" or even "to My

Word." Jesus Himself is the only true Fountain who can quench our thirst, and we must move forward into His presence.

On this three-word invitation from Jesus, J. Oswald Sanders has these comments:

> Christ is claiming the ability to satisfy the deepest need of the human heart, yet we are strangely reluctant to come directly to Him. We will attend ceremonies and observe sacraments. We will follow men and congregate in meetings. We will frequent camps and conventions. We will listen to priests and preachers—anything, it would seem, except come personally and alone into the presence of Christ. But He is absolutely intolerant. He will quench our spiritual thirst personally and not by proxy.[8]

Only the sweet comingling of His presence with our spirits can bring the watering our souls cry out for.

The verb tense for "come" in John 7:37 carries the idea of a continual coming. Christ never intended us to come, take one drink from Him for salvation, then continue on our way until He takes us to heaven. He created this deep thirst in us and desires us to come continually to Him, pressing past all distractions, so we can drink greedily from the water He alone provides.

Of course it's one thing to come to Him; it's another thing to drink. I can come to a water fountain when I'm thirsty, but that isn't the same as actually drinking. Only when I bend over and drink the cold water will my thirst be remedied.

Too often in life I've spent time coming to Christ but not really drinking. It happened this morning. Feeling the pressure of completing this manuscript, I felt justified in skimping on my time alone with Him (though I dare not miss it altogether, lest He not bless my writing of this book!). So though I did spend time with Him, it was just sort of "touching base." I gave Him my prayer requests, thanked Him for His blessings, asked Him to bless the missionaries, then proceeded on my way. I touched the fringes of His garments but failed to enter into penetrating and transforming communion with His Person. (Maybe, just maybe, you know what I'm talking about from your own experience.)

Yet so much more is available to us! "In Your presence is fullness of joy; at Your right hand are pleasures forevermore" (Psalm 16:11). But this fullness and pleasure require drinking. Only in drinking can we powerfully experience and richly taste the Person of Christ, so that our souls thrill with delight and our lives begin to reflect the undeniable evidence of being with Jesus.

What, then, does it mean to drink?

Drinking is not sipping, which is what too many of us are doing in our relationship with Christ. To drink is to passionately appropriate the living waters, to eagerly seize them for one's own.

To the degree we're drinking from other cisterns, we can only sip from God's fountain. We'll be caught in the deadlock with God that George MacDonald described: "Man finds it hard to get what he wants, because he does not want the best; God finds it hard to give, because He would give the best, and man does not want it."[9] When we fail to recognize that what we most deeply want is often far more and far better than what we think we want, we settle for secondary waters. And in settling for secondary waters, there isn't enough room in our mouths to enjoy the best water, which only God can provide.

But when we refuse to diminish our thirst at counterfeit wells, we'll come to our Lord in the fullness of need, and we'll deeply, genuinely drink. We'll open our mouths wide, gulp greedily all the water we can get hold of, and keep intently drinking until our thirst is quenched.

How is it with you, my friend? Are you drinking or sipping? Are you coming to your Lord with burning neediness or casual interest? Most often the answer will be in accord with the number of broken cisterns we're frequenting.

DYNAMIC CONDUITS

What are the different components of spiritual drinking? Does it mean reading our Bibles? praying? fasting? taking communion?

Well, yes and no. It all depends on the reason those things are done and the energy behind them. When they're done as a means of obligating God to bless us or as a demonstration to Him, to others, and to ourselves of how spiritual we are, these "spiritual disciplines" become mere trinkets of fleshly religiosity. They impart nothing to the soul except a false sense of spiritual superiority or security.

But when these same things are done to draw near to God Himself, seeking not His hand but His face, they become dynamic conduits for the life of God to our souls. The passionate pursuit and glad enjoyment of Christ in our souls is the essence of drinking, and how this is done can vary dramatically from person to person. But the end is always the same— slaking our God-created thirst in the rivers of Christ's life-invigorating presence.

The verb for *drink* in John 7:37 (like that for *come*) is in a tense that signifies repeated action—drinking again and again. We can never drink too often or too deeply of Christ's rivers. Our drinking was never intended to be a once-in-a-lifetime or even a once-every-twenty-four-hours affair, but an hour-by-hour, minute-by-minute, second-by-second kind of on-going appropriation of the Person of Christ. This word *drink* is synonymous with *believe* in verse 38. God never intended for our faith in Christ to be a sporadic, on-again, off-again affair, and the same is true about our spiritual drinking.

We cannot represent heaven on earth well until we ourselves have become heavenly connoisseurs. Until our thirst has been slaked by rivers of living waters, it will be difficult to recommend those waters to others. As John Stott writes,

> Nothing shuts the mouth, seals the lips, and ties the tongue like the secret poverty of our own spiritual experience. We do not bear witness for the simple reason that we have no witness to bear.... If the Bread of life has evidently not satisfied us, why should non-Christians suppose it will satisfy them?[10]

When we've drunk so deeply of the life of Christ that our souls are moist with the delightful sense of His presence, then we, too, will echo the sentiments of the early disciples: "For we cannot but speak the things which we have seen and heard" (Acts 4:20). Our evangelism will be as Robert Munger described it: "the spontaneous overflow of a glad and free heart in Jesus Christ."[11]

RELATIONSHIP MORE THAN SERVICE

Becoming a heavenly connoisseur is what C. S. Lewis was getting at when he said our "Christian duty" is "for everyone to be as happy as he can"—meaning, "as happy *in God* as we can be."[12] This is what John Piper refers to as "Christian hedonism," a concept that's not only thoroughly biblical, but vitally important for at least three reasons.

It's important first because of God's preeminent calling upon our lives. That calling has to do with our relationship with Him, not our service for Him. From Genesis to Revelation we find that God's relentless pursuit of man has far more to do with taking hold of his heart than enlisting his hand. What delights Him far more than a morally upright life or one spent in service to others is a life caught up in passionate pursuit of knowing and enjoying Him. He rebukes the doctrinally correct, ministry-laden church of Ephesus for not giving Him what He values most of all: "You have left your first love" (Revelation 2:4). He commends Mary for choosing "that good part, which will never be taken away from her" (Luke 10:42)—that intimacy and enjoyment of Christ.

Each of us must make a fundamental decision if our lives are to have God's anointing upon them: Will we make *knowing* God more important than *serving* Him? Knowing Him isn't *as* important, but *more.* It's more important because ministry is always the spillover of the fullness of Christ's life from within; Christ calls us to drink before we can flow. Knowing Him is more important because we won't recognize the ways He wants to flow through us unless we've spent time at His feet learning His ways.

Most of all, it's more important because it's more important *to Him,* though I freely admit I still don't fully understand that. Somehow the God who holds the universe in the palm of His hand, who lifts up islands as if they were grains of sands, who keeps meticulous track of the stars in the sky and the hairs on our heads—this same God would rather have the enjoyment of our company than the labor of our ministry.

Our being delighted in God is also important because of what it means for God's reputation. It isn't just obedience God is after, but Christ-scented obedience. Ellen Glasgow wrote of her father, a Presbyterian elder, "He was entirely unselfish and in his long life he never committed a pleasure." Oliver Wendell Holmes noted, "I might have entered the ministry if certain clergymen I knew had not looked and acted so much like undertakers." Ministry that's drained of joy and stiffly carried out in dutiful obedience betrays the God it purports to represent.

"The Christian owes it to the world to be supernaturally joyful," Tozer wrote.[13] This doesn't mean a spiritual facade that plasters Pollyanna smiles over deep internal pain. True Christianity meets the realities of living in a fallen world head on, without pretending or denying. However, it meets them with another set of realities, divine ones, including a joy that can't be explained. This joy doesn't eliminate pain and heartache; it resides alongside these things, giving us new strength to press on and reminding us that we're temporary aliens in this world.

Why is our abiding joy so important for God's reputation? John Piper gives the reason:

> God's deepest purpose for the world is to fill it with reverberations of His glory in the lives of a new humanity, ransomed from every people, tribe, tongue, and nation (Revelation 5:9). But the glory of God does not reflect brightly in the hearts of men and women when they cower unwillingly in submission to His authority or when they obey in servile fear or when there is no gladness in their response to their King.
>
> God's aim is not to constrain men's submission by an act of raw authority, His aim is to ravish their affections with irresistible displays of His glory. The only submission that fully reflects the worth and glory of the King is glad submission. No gladness in the subject, no glory to the King.[14]

Drinking deeply is vital not only for what it does for our own souls, but even more for what it does in putting God's name on display.

Being happy and satisfied in God is also important because of the inbred longings of our new heart. One of our great promises from God in the New Covenant is this one: "I will give them a heart to know Me" (Jeremiah 24:7). Our desire to know God is wholly gifted to us at our conversion. It isn't up to us to create a longing to know God, but to nurture and stimulate the already gifted longings supernaturally implanted within.

Why should you drink deeply from Christ's waters? Let me give you a reason you might not have considered: because you *want* to! At the deepest level of your being is a God-grafted yearning to know Him that can never be eradicated or extinguished. Certainly it can be neglected, quenched, or covered over by other competing passions. But it will never, ever go away.

Christ has made you a God-lover through the new heart He placed within you (see Ezekiel 36:26), and you'll never find the vibrant rest your soul longs for until you allow your new, God-given desires to carry you back to the Source from whom they came. "Oh, taste and see that the LORD is good; blessed is the man who trusts in Him!" (Psalm 34:8).

OUR CONSUMING DESIRE

Drink deeply, flow freely. Those four words come close to summarizing the whole of the Christian life. And their order can't be violated: To be able to flow freely requires that we first be drinking deeply.

Are you drinking deeply, child of God? I didn't ask if you were studying your Bible, or praying, or serving, but something far more important: Are you allowing your raging thirst to be slaked at His waters? Are you pressing on to know firsthand His ravishing beauty, His loving heart, and His eternal ways?

May our great, consuming pursuit in life be that of David, the man after God's own heart: "One thing I have desired of the LORD, that will I seek: that I may dwell in the house of the LORD all the days of my life, to behold the beauty of the LORD, and to inquire in His temple" (Psalm 27:4).

"My principal enjoyment," wrote Henry Martyn, a missionary to the Muslim world two hundred years ago, "is the enjoyment of His presence."[15] In our day as well, everything about becoming a river of God hinges upon this being our chief pursuit in life. It's simply coming back home to what we've always longed for most—whether we were aware of it or not.

Supernatural Influencers

Make me Thy fuel, Flame of God.
AMY CARMICHAEL

It had happened again. As I walked back to my hotel room, I found myself deeply stirred to want to know God in new and fresh ways. Once I was inside the room, opening my Bible seemed more alluring than turning on the television. I also felt a tugging at my heart to begin taking certain risks that God was calling me to but that I had been resisting.

This stirring felt wonderfully clean and invigorating, wholly independent of any working on my part. It was unmistakably the movement of the Holy Spirit. How had it happened?

One of my closest friends and I were leading a conference together in Wisconsin. We were both tired after the evening session, and before going to bed we stopped at the hotel restaurant for a quick bite. Our intent was to eat quickly, but as we started talking, my friend began asking questions that led to an extended discussion about where we both were in our walks with God and relationships with others. He's a skilled and gifted counselor, but not once did he convey the sense of being "on duty." Our conversation had an ebb and flow that seemed both energized and relaxed at the same time. I can only say it felt anointed.

This wasn't the first time I'd experienced this with him. More times than

I can count, God has used him over the years to pour deeply into my soul. Many times I've left his presence praying, "God, help me to know You more deeply" and "Help me to take the risks I know You're calling me to take."

IS GOD DOING IT?

Men and women who can stimulate this kind of Godward stirring in other believers are what I call "supernatural influencers." They have impact on others in ways only God makes possible.

All of us have a certain degree of influence on others, but how much of it is genuinely supernatural? Is our life a testimony to the abilities of our well-trained flesh, or is there impact that can't be explained apart from divine indwelling? If God were to withdraw His Spirit from this world, how much of our life would continue unhindered and how much would come to a screeching halt?

Or is this issue even something to be bothered with? Maybe we should follow the common advice of our day and just "do what's right." Why worry about whether it's God doing it or us?

But isn't there something within you, my friend, that yearns to know your life has been part of something that absolutely required God?

Of course there is, if you're truly listening to your new heart. Your deeply implanted, Spirit-breathed longings cry out for that unmistakable sense of being carried along in a movement of God. Nothing on the face of the earth compares with the deep thrill of knowing we're part of something that can be credited only to God.

Tragically, too few Christians taste this thrill.

I once heard a prominent Christian leader talk about the church growth conferences he was helping lead many weekends each year. As he was flying home one Sunday night, it occurred to Him that everything he'd taught that weekend would work just as well for the Kiwanis Club as for the church. Nothing blatantly supernatural characterized his recommendations for that church to grow; nothing absolutely required God. This piercing revelation launched him into a new search for the kind of ministry that could be done only in God.

Radically God and Radically Good

So what sets apart those who really are "supernatural influencers" from those who are working from their own strength?

Supernatural influencers are men and women living in vital communion with God, desperately depending upon His resources, and yielding to His flow through their lives. They aren't trying to make something happen *for* God; they're jealous to see that what escapes from their lives is something *God* has caused to happen.

They may or may not have formal theological training or great intellectual abilities. They may or may not have charismatic personalities or natural leadership abilities. They may or may not have high standing in society or celebrity status, be it in sports, music, acting, politics, or whatever. God is neither bound nor impressed by any of these things.

What they do have is brokenness of spirit and confidence in Christ that He alone will do *through* them whatever He has required *from* them.

Certainly, there can be no better model of supernatural influence than our Lord Jesus Christ. Peter sums up marvelously the whole of His life with these words: "God anointed Jesus of Nazareth with the Holy Spirit and with power, who went about doing good and healing all who were oppressed by the devil, for God was with Him" (Acts 10:38).

We observe first in this passage that supernatural influence is radically dependent on God's presence. God Himself anointed Jesus with the Holy Spirit and power. Jesus' entire life was a fragrant testimony to His radical distrust in His own native abilities. "I can of Myself do nothing," He declared (John 5:30). What was the secret to His life? Christ Himself gives the answer: "The Father who dwells in Me does the works" (John 14:10). Jesus lived the most dynamic life ever lived *because He lived the most dependent life ever lived.*

So must it be with us. Christ said in no uncertain terms, "Without Me you can do nothing" (John 15:5). There isn't the slightest hint of exaggeration in these words. All gifts, talents, and abilities are useless in terms of eternal significance unless they're brought under the sway and control of the Holy Spirit. Natural assets can never accomplish supernatural purposes on their own.

Samuel Brengle, one of the early leaders of the Salvation Army, understood this well. One night he was introduced to speak as the "great Dr. Brengle." That night he wrote in his diary,

> If I appear great in their eyes, the Lord is most graciously helping me to see how absolutely nothing I am without Him, and helping me to keep little in my own eyes. He does use me. But I am so concerned that He uses me and that it is not of me the work is done. The axe cannot boast of the trees it has cut down. It could do nothing but for the woodsman. He made it, he sharpened it, and he used it. The moment he throws it aside, it becomes only old iron. O, that I may never lose sight of this.[1]

In *Spiritual Leadership*, J. Oswald Sanders pointed out the differences between natural and spiritual influence (please see the chart on the next page).[2] He observed that a spiritual leader influences others,

> not by the power of his own personality alone but by that personality irradiated, interpenetrated, and empowered by the Holy Spirit. Because he permits the Holy Spirit undisputed control in his life, the Spirit's power can flow unhindered through him to others.[3]

The older I get, the more I long to know that whatever influence God allows me to have upon others is genuinely of Him. I can't think of many things I'd rather have spoken at my funeral than this: "Dwight's life can't be explained apart from the power of God."

My guess is that you want the same. Why not take a moment right now and ask God to grant this to you, whatever the cost? And while you're at it, would you pray the same thing for your pastor?

Your Vocation of Ministry

Something else to notice from Peter's words about Christ is that supernatural influencers see all of life as an opportunity for ministry. How beautifully Peter summarized the life of our Lord: "He went about doing good." Jesus didn't do good only when He was in the synagogue or while teaching

The Differences Between Natural and Spiritual Influence

NATURAL LEADER	SPIRITUAL LEADER
Self-confident	Confident in God
Knows men	Also knows God
Makes own decisions	Seeks to find God's will
Ambitious	Self-effacing (humble)
Originates own methods	Finds and follows God's methods
Enjoys commanding others	Delights to obey God
Motivated by personal considerations	Motivated by love for God and others
Independent	Dependent

or while ministering to the crowds. He was always "on" for serving and helping others; there were no boundaries to it. He just went about doing the will of His Father in whatever arena He happened to be.

No dichotomy exists between *ministry* and *lifestyle.* All of life is an opportunity for ministry, and there's no situation or setting in which God doesn't desire to be made known. "Whether you eat or drink, or whatever you do, do all to the glory of God" (1 Corinthians 10:31). This passage sets the boundaries for where ministry is to take place: all of life, in every place, at all times.

Ministry isn't a slotted time frame of activity such as preaching, teaching Sunday school, or going out on visitation. It's allowing God to flow through us in whatever way He chooses and in whatever setting He places us.

To think through this, consider the following:

Which is more spiritual…

preaching on Sunday morning	or	eating lunch with friends afterward?
teaching Sunday school	or	coaching little league baseball?
going to seminary	or	going to law school?
being pastor of a church	or	being a garbage collector?
being a missionary in Africa	or	being a golf pro in Palm Springs?
going on a mission trip	or	going on a ski vacation?
attending a Bible study group	or	attending a Rotary Club meeting?
being on the elder board	or	being on the school board?

What's the right answer? In each pairing, either option could be the correct answer; it all depends on what God has called you to. If He has called you to be a golf pro in Palm Springs, then going as a missionary to Africa would be the fleshly thing to do. You were called to be a missionary in Palm Springs through golf, and going elsewhere would be an avoidance of

God's best for you. The same would be true about being a golf pro if God instead had called you to be a missionary to Africa.

True ministry isn't primarily about occupation or location, but about a Spirit-compelled lifestyle that permeates all of our existence. Occupation and location are secondary to the far greater issue of the lordship of Christ in every area of life.

One of the great burdens I have for the body of Christ is for believers to understand and embrace the great reality that we're all in full-time Christian service. We have different disguises, but the same vocation: to be out-and-out lovers and servants of the Lord Jesus.

When I graduated from college, I was offered a job as a tennis pro in Midland, Texas. After praying about it, I became convinced this was where God wanted to use me. I moved to Midland not as a tennis pro, but as a disciple of Christ disguised as a tennis pro. Those were great years, and I got to share my faith with many people who would never listen to me now as a pastor.

A few years later, God moved me to a new ministry position in the church where I'm still serving. But I don't feel that what I'm doing now is one iota more spiritual than what I was doing back then as a tennis pro. Based on the Word of God as well as my personal experience, I don't sense that what I was doing before was only part-time Christian work and that now I'm full-time. I was in full-time ministry in Midland, and I'm in full-time ministry today. There's no such thing as secular jobs versus sacred jobs. The only difference is the occupational label. The vocation has remained identical.

Where are you, my friend? Do you understand that your occupation is only a temporary platform for your vocation? Your vocation will always remain the same—to glorify God. You're in full-time Christian service no matter what your job is. And what determines the significance of your life isn't how much "church work" you're involved in, but whether you're going about doing good for the glory of God wherever you are.

The ramifications of this are staggering. It means that each day is filled with occasions for spiritual influence. From the neighbor next door to the secretary at work to the clerk at the counter to the trainer at the gym—all are divinely orchestrated opportunities to exert spiritual influence through glorifying God, even though we won't necessarily see the influence we're having.

Our calling, therefore, is not to go out and find a place where we can make an impact for God, but to abandon ourselves to a life of abiding in Christ and then, like our Lord, to simply go around and do whatever good God directs and empowers us toward.

Maybe this sounds heavy to you—to think of living every moment of life under the yoke of being "on" for God. But it doesn't mean we don't take time off, as our Lord did, for our spiritual, emotional, mental, and physical recharging. You'll find from the Scriptures, however, and from your own new heart, that total abandonment to God is what you were made for. Nothing will satisfy you more deeply. And attacking life this way brings such a wonderful simplicity, freedom, and joy. It will revolutionize how you approach life and ministry.

Sitting down with a friend over coffee is every bit as spiritual as going to church together. That casual setting provides just as great an opportunity for supernatural influence as being in church does—and often even more.

Every believer has something of great significance to offer because we all have the treasure of God's indwelling presence in our "earthen vessels" (2 Corinthians 4:7), and whenever this indwelling treasure is brought out into the open, ministry takes place, whether in a Sunday-school room or a locker room.

LET THE FRAGRANCE DO ITS JOB

But how does this supernatural influence take place? One of the most crucial aspects of supernaturally influencing others is this: *Our greatest impact upon others often comes when we're not intentionally trying to have impact upon them.* The unconscious impression we leave on others is often the most powerful.

We know what it is to consciously seek to influence others. It may be giving instructions to a new coworker, giving advice to a friend, or lecturing our child. Or in my case, teaching on Sunday morning to get across the truths of God's Word. All these are examples of conscious, intended impact. But another kind of impact often is the most powerful. It takes place when our guard is down, when we've gone "off duty," when we're oblivious to the fact that anyone is watching.

This kind of impact is described in 2 Corinthians 2:14-16:

Now thanks be to God who always leads us in triumph in Christ, and through us diffuses the fragrance of His knowledge in every place. For we are to God the fragrance of Christ among those who are being saved and among those who are perishing. To the one we are the aroma of death leading to death, and to the other the aroma of life leading to life.

Note here the source of the impact: fragrance. The aroma of Christ. We don't put on perfume or cologne, then go out and work at smelling good. No, we relax in the scent of the perfume or cologne upon us; we just let it do its job. So it is spiritually. As we live in vital union with our resurrected Lord, the unmistakable sense of His presence lingers heavily upon us. God Himself "diffuses through us" this scent of heaven. And it's strong enough to either draw or repel, depending upon the heart of each person around us.

This fragrance includes at least nine different scents: "love, joy, peace, longsuffering, kindness, goodness, faithfulness, gentleness, self-control" (Galatians 5:22-23). This is what one man has aptly called a "whiff of heaven." It's the somewhat intangible, yet undeniable sense that God has drawn near. Yet this fragrance is never self-generated; it's the unavoidable result of a life spent lingering in the presence of God. This is what J. Oswald Sanders was getting at when he wrote, "True spirituality is the diffused fragrance that has been assimilated in the garden of the Lord."[4]

The Aroma of Radical Faith

One of the great examples of the power of unconscious impression is found in the conversion of the nineteenth-century journalist Henry Stanley. An atheist, Stanley was hired to do a story on the famous missionary David Livingstone and spent extended time with him in the jungles of Africa. There he came to trust Christ himself after observing the following:

> You may take any point of Dr. Livingstone's character, and analyze it carefully, and I would challenge any man to find a fault in it.... His gentleness never forsakes him; his hopefulness never deserts him. No harassing anxieties, distraction of mind, long separation from home and kindred, can make him complain.... His religion is not of the theoretical kind, but is a constant, earnest, sincere practice. It is neither demonstrative or loud, but manifests itself in a quiet practical way, and is always at work.... In him religion exhibits its loveliest features; it governs his conduct not only towards his servants but toward the natives, the bigoted Mohammedans, and all who come in contact with him.[5]

This is the essence of unconscious impression. It's a life lived preeminently before God, and it leaks out before men. The leaks are where the impact on others can most often be forcefully felt.

This poem expresses it well:

Not only in the words you say,
Not only in your deeds confessed,
But in the most unconscious way
Is Christ expressed.
For me 'twas not the truth you taught,
To you so clear, to me so dim;
But when you came to me,
You brought a sense of Him.
And from your eyes He beckons me,
And from your heart His love is shed,
Till I lose sight of you
And see the living Christ instead.[6]

As you read those lines, does something within you rise up to say, "Yes, that's what I want my life to be about"? That something is the Holy Spirit, working through your new heart. You were redeemed for nothing short of this kind of blatantly supernatural life, and you'll be deeply satisfied with nothing less.

This indeed is the transforming power of true godly living.

Larry Crabb's father was a godly, committed laborer in the Plymouth Brethren church. By occupation he was an electrical worker; by vocation, an all-out disciple of Christ. Larry recalls that in his boyhood their family enjoyed gathering around to watch the Red Skelton comedy program on television. This was one of the highlights of their week. Larry recalls one occasion when he ran into his father's study to let him know the show was about to begin. His dad looked up from his Bible, and in a kind but disinterested way said, "Go on, son, and enjoy the show. I think I'll miss it this time."

Larry left in awe, wondering what kind of God this must be to get his dad to read the Bible and pray and forgo Red Skelton. Surely there must be something he hadn't latched on to yet in this thing called Christianity.

Now Larry's dad wasn't waiting in his study, hoping his son would come in so he could teach him a lesson on priorities. He was walking humbly before His God, relishing the things of the Spirit, and letting the chips fall where they might. When life is lived in this vein, the chips tend to fall in powerful directions.

I could give you example after example of this. Often when I've told men who mentored me about the things they did to impact me, they can't remember what I'm talking about. They were living radically before God, and I just happened to be in their presence when He broke through. Their focus was on knowing and serving God, not on ministering to me, and this is precisely why He used them to impact me so deeply.

The Unmistakable Scent of Jesus

What does it take to have the fragrance of Christ hanging heavy upon us, so His presence is unmistakably featured in our lives?

I can think of no better answer than to look back at two of the greatest influencers in church history, Peter and John. They were summoned before the religious leaders of their day, and when those leaders "saw the boldness of Peter and John, and perceived that they were uneducated and untrained men, they marveled. And they realized that they had been with Jesus" (Acts 4:13).

How did they know Peter and John had been with Jesus? Were they wearing a cross, or a fish, or a WWJD bracelet? Obviously not. What they saw was a glad exuberance ("the boldness") reminding them unmistakably of Jesus. It was the diffused fragrance of the Lord that came from extended, firsthand intimacy with Him.

As I look back on my conversion, the power of unconscious influence was one of the things God used most mightily to bring me to Christ. Our high school had a number of what we called "Jesus freaks" (looking back, I think they were just regular Christians). One of them, David Cobb, was a fullback on the football team and an outstanding student. While he wasn't shy about his faith, at the same time he wasn't preachy or pushy, nor was he judgmental or condescending toward us pagans. He was always available to help me in classes we had together.

I couldn't figure David out. There was something about him I found attractive and puzzling at the same time. Here was a guy who could have had so many of the sinful pleasures I longed for, yet he was passing them up. And he had a joy in his life that I knew was missing in mine.

David never shared the gospel with me; I don't remember there ever being an appropriate opportunity. Yet his unconscious influence was one of the biggest reasons I became a believer. He was a wonderful example of the words of Francis of Assisi: "Preach the gospel at all times. If necessary, use words."

This is the heartbeat of being a supernatural influencer. And it's available to all of us.

The Main Thing

His likeness to Christ is the truth of a man....
As Christ is the blossom of humanity, so the blossom
of every man is the Christ perfected in him.
GEORGE MACDONALD

A few years ago I was attempting to help my wife with the gardening around our house. She pointed out to me a flower bed that needed weeding, and I quickly went to work with great diligence, extracting all the weeds I could find. By the time I'd finished there were no weeds to be found anywhere.

With great delight in my accomplishment, I invited my wife to come over and marvel in what a great job I'd done. The expression on her face quickly told me she wasn't as impressed as I had hoped. In fact, it told me that I probably would have been better off not helping at all. She let me know I'd extracted not just the weeds but also most of the flowers. (I'm still not sure how to tell the difference.)

An important lesson was reinforced for me that day: Know exactly what you're aiming for. Be sure about what things to attack, what things to leave alone, and what things to nurture.

As we continue our exploration of what it means to supernaturally influence others, this same model holds true as well. God wants to use each of us as His personal conduit to powerfully pour Himself through us into others' lives. Our influence will have the touch of God upon it only as we cooperate with what He's seeking to do through us.

A significant part of this cooperating with God is a Spirit-wrought sensitivity to what things need to be confronted, what things need to be left alone, and what things need to be strengthened and nurtured. But most of all, it's crucial to know specifically what target *God* is aiming at in working through us. If we don't begin with the proper end in mind, we'll be in grave danger of becoming a religious success but a spiritual failure.

HELPING OTHERS BECOME LIKE JESUS

What, then, is the true goal of spirituality, the crosshairs to aim for in impacting others? The Bible hasn't stuttered on this issue, but speaks with unmistakable clarity:

> He also predestined [us] to be *conformed to the image of His Son.* (Romans 8:29)

> My little children, for whom I labor in birth again until *Christ is formed in you.* (Galatians 4:19)

> Him we preach…that we may present every man *perfect* [complete] *in Christ Jesus.* (Colossians 1:28)

It can be said in different ways, but it all comes back to the same central issue, as C. S. Lewis observed:

> It is so easy to think that the Church has a lot of different objects—education, building, missions, holding services.… *The Church exists for nothing else but to draw men into Christ, to make them little Christs.* If they are not doing that, all the cathedrals, missions, sermons, even

the Bible itself, are simply a waste of time. God became man for no
other purpose.[1] (emphasis mine)

I like to put it this way: The goal of our spiritual influence on others is
to cooperate with God in helping them fulfill their whole potential in
Christ. It's to be used by God to help others become more like Jesus.

I'm struck, though, by how insipid the phrase *becoming like Christ* has
become in our day. We think of Christlikeness in such safe, mellow,
unthreatening terms that it would seem God is calling us to a life of little
more than maxed-out niceness. When we say God wants us to become
like His Son, do we have any idea of how radical a proposition this is? On
deep reflection, it would seem far easier to harness the sun, seize the stars,
and drink the ocean than to become like God's Son.

Listen to the words of Dorothy L. Sayers:

I believe it is a grave mistake to present Christianity as something
charming and popular with no offense in it.... We cannot blink the
fact that Jesus meek and mild was so stiff in His opinions and so
inflammatory in His language that He was thrown out of church,
stoned, hunted from place to place, and finally gibbeted as a firebrand and a public danger. Whatever His peace was, it was not the
peace of an amiable indifference.

Later she adds,

The people who hanged Christ never, to do them justice, accused
Him of being a bore—on the contrary, they thought Him too
dynamic to be safe. It has been left for later generations to muffle up
that shattering personality and surround Him with an atmosphere of
tedium. We have very efficiently pared the claws of the Lion of Judah,
certified Him "meek and mild" and recommended Him as a fitting

household pet for pale curates and pious old ladies. Those who
knew Him, however…objected to Him as a dangerous firebrand.[2]

If the real Jesus were to walk among us today, He would be every bit
as controversial as He was back then. He wouldn't be welcome in a great
number of churches. He would once again attack the superficiality and
hypocrisy of many religious leaders, He would mingle dangerously close
with prostitutes and drug dealers, and He would go places most religious
people won't.

Let's face it: The Jesus of the New Testament and the Jesus presented
by today's churches are often not the same Person. So if people are going
to catch a glimpse of the Jesus of the New Testament—the real Jesus—
where can they look?

The best place is in the Gospels (and the rest of Scripture), where the
true Christ is seen in living color and unadulterated reality. But they probably won't look there until they first catch sight of Jesus in you and me and
others who call themselves *Christians* (after all, the word literally means
"little Christs"). It's through the medium of faltering, frail humanity that
God has designed His Son to be most powerfully exhibited in our time.
Most people will never want to read about Christ in the Gospels until they
first see Him revealed in our own lives.

Nothing can be more *radical* or *impossible* than becoming like
Christ—radical because no one has ever lived in the utterly abandoned,
God-dependent, others-centered way that He did. He gave us not just a
fleeting glimpse of the Father, but the full voltage of incarnated deity. He
was "*full* of grace and truth" (John 1:14).

G. Walter Hansen sees a great disparity in comparing his own passion
with what Christ displayed:

I am spellbound by the intensity of Jesus' emotions—not a twinge
of pity, but heartbroken compassion; not a passing irritation, but

terrifying anger; not a silent tear, but groans of anguish; not a weak smile, but ecstatic celebration. Jesus' emotions are like a mountain river cascading with clear water. My emotions are more like a muddy foam or a feeble trickle.[3]

In our emotional intensity as well as in every other aspect, becoming like Christ is so utterly beyond our own capabilities that it requires supernatural enablement for any hope of even partial success.

What then does Christlikeness genuinely look like? And what does it *not* look like?

For me, a particularly meaningful answer to those questions is found in the image of a tree, which is used often in Scripture to picture true spirituality (as in Psalm 1:3; 92:12-15; Jeremiah 17:7-8; Hosea 14:4-8).

Three central aspects characterize this image of the tree, and they also characterized the life of our Lord—*deep roots, supernatural fruit,* and *extending branches.* As I think of spiritual growth in my own life as well as in others, this is the image I go back to again and again.

DEEP ROOTS

Nothing is more important to the life of a tree than its root system. The roots anchor the tree and bring it nourishment. Look at just a few passages related to roots in the Scriptures:

> You…caused it to take deep root,
> And it filled the land. (Psalm 80:9)

> The root of the righteous yields fruit. (Proverbs 12:12)

> Blessed is the man who trusts in the LORD
> And whose hope is the LORD.

For he shall be like a tree planted by the waters,
Which spreads out its roots by the river. (Jeremiah 17:7-8)

Ephraim is stricken,
Their root is dried up;
They shall bear no fruit. (Hosea 9:16)

And they have no root in themselves, and so endure only for a time.
(Mark 4:17)

So walk in Him, rooted and built up in Him. (Colossians 2:6-7)

The roots determine everything—the health, the beauty, the size, the stability, and the endurance of the tree. In *Root of the Righteous*, A. W. Tozer notes,

> The bough that breaks off from the tree in a storm may bloom briefly and give to the unthinking passer-by the impression that it is a healthy and fruitful branch, but its tender blossoms will soon perish and the bough itself wither and die. *There is no lasting life apart from the root.* Much that passes for Christianity today is the brief bright effort of the severed branch to bring forth its fruit in its season. Preoccupation with appearances and a corresponding neglect of the out-of-sight root of the spiritual life are prophetic signs which go unheeded.[4] (emphasis mine)

Nowhere is this seen more forcefully than in the life of our Lord. "So He Himself often withdrew into the wilderness and prayed" (Luke 5:16). Not only did He spend protracted time alone with His Father, He drew upon His Father's life continually during the course of each day. "But the Father who dwells in Me does the works" (John 14:10).

I'm intrigued by the fact that the specifics of our Lord's root system are so sparsely described. Other than praying and one instance of fasting, we aren't given specifics of what He did during His time alone with God. Did He sing? meditate on Scripture? fast? journal? We simply don't know.

I think there's a good reason for this. Deepening our roots into God is an intensely relational endeavor. If we knew more of the specifics of what our Lord did, our flesh would immediately gravitate toward pursuing those activities rather than the Lord Himself. We would turn them into mechanical disciplines for proving our spirituality or obligating God to bless us.

Having deep roots means *a life of ongoing and deepening cultivation of the Person and presence of God.* It's the white-hot pursuit and the glad finding of intimacy with each member of the Godhead.

Wholehearted Pursuit of God

David gave us a poignant and exquisite expression of what this means: "One thing I have desired of the LORD, that will I seek: that I may dwell in the house of the LORD all the days of my life, to behold the beauty of the LORD, and to inquire in His temple" (Psalm 27:4). This single verse powerfully sums up so much of what I believe it means to cultivate a life of deep roots.

Note first the priority of David's pursuit: He desired and sought "one thing" of the Lord. He clearly knew what he wanted more than anything else from God.

How about you, my friend? If God promised to grant you one request and no more, what would you ask for?

Think about it. If you'll listen closely to the stirrings of your new heart within, you'll hear what you most want—and most need. From the depths of your being comes an undeniable yearning that what you want most from God...is God. His face, His smile, His communion, His friendship, His presence.

These are the things He has caused you to value above all else. "I will give them a heart to know Me" (Jeremiah 24:7) is the promise of God and the work of God at your conversion. The moment you came to Christ, He placed within your spirit a hunger and thirst for knowing Him personally and deeply. This upward longing can never be deadened or eradicated, though it often gets covered over by other competing passions of the flesh. Ultimately though, what we yearn for most deeply from God, just as David did, is to dwell in His house, beholding His splendor and relishing His friendship.

Augustine once asked himself what it was about God that he loved.

Not physical beauty…or the radiance of light that pleases the eye,
or the sweet melody of old familiar songs, or the fragrance of flowers
and ointments and spices…. None of these do I love when I love
my God. Yet there is a kind of light, and a kind of melody, and a
kind of fragrance, and a kind of food, and a kind of embracing
when I love my God. They are the kind of light and sound and
odor and food and love that affect the senses of the inner man….
It hears melodies that never fade with time. It inhales lovely scents
that are not blown away by the wind. It eats without diminishing
or consuming the supply. It never gets separated from the embrace
of God and never gets tired of it. That is what I love when I love
my God.[5]

More often than we would like, our pursuit of God is for His hand rather than His face. In such moments we're seeking Him for His circumstantial blessings. This isn't to say it's wrong to pray specifically for God's provisions in our lives. Scripture, in fact, calls us to that. The issue, rather, is one of priority: What do we want *most* from God?

In this same psalm David cried out, "When You said, 'Seek My face,' my heart said to You, 'Your face, LORD, I will seek'" (Psalm 27:8). Men and women with deep roots value God's face above anything else on earth, even the legitimate provisions of His hand.

I'm also impressed by how David's words reflect his firsthand experience of this pursuit—"that I may dwell *in* the house of the Lord all the days of my life." David wasn't content to know *about* the God who dwelt in the tabernacle; he pushed past the hindrances and distractions to find a front-row seat to behold and enjoy Yahweh personally.

It's one thing to know the various theological categories concerning the attributes of God; it's a very different thing to experience those attributes firsthand. One can have intellectual realization without ever having experiential realization. To be experiential there must be a heart-level connection.

For instance, my mind may be utterly convinced that God is love, as the Scriptures say, while at the same time my heart may be utterly devoid of experiencing that love. I can know the Bible says God is holy without my inner self ever being stirred by His holiness.

Along these lines, Jonathan Edwards writes,

> Thus there is a difference between having an *opinion* that God is holy and gracious, and having a *sense* of the loveliness and beauty of that holiness and grace. There is a difference between having a rational judgment that honey is sweet, and having a sense of its sweetness. A man may have the former, that knows not how honey tastes; but a man cannot have the latter unless he has an idea of the taste of honey in his mind.[6]

Men and women with deep roots aren't content to read in their Bibles about the sweetness, majesty, and awesomeness of God; they want to behold and seize and taste these things for themselves.

This is what the Puritan Stephen Charnock meant by "using the attributes of God." Deep-rooted saints aren't willing to be told about the mountain of God; they press upward to climb it for themselves, to scale its heights and breathe its rarified air and become intoxicated with its beauty. They wholeheartedly agree with these words from Frederick W. Faber:

> Only to sit and think of God;
> O what a joy it is.
> To think the thought,
> To breathe the Name,
> Earth hath no higher bliss.[7]

A Worshiper and a Learner

We also see the goal of David's pursuit: "to behold the beauty of the LORD, and to inquire in His temple" (Psalm 27:4).

I'm struck by the wonderful balance found here in his pursuit of God. He came as both a worshiper ("to behold the beauty of the Lord") and a learner ("to inquire in His temple"). He desired to be ravished by the sight of God's stunning beauty and blazing perfection. He also longed to know more and more fully the ways and wisdom of His Lord.

Churches and individual Christians today focus too often on one of these to the neglect of the other. For some, it's preoccupation with passion for God through worship (which is seen primarily as music); what matters most is for their hearts to be touched and stirred by the encounter. Others are instead absorbed with sound Bible doctrine, and what matters most to them is to have their minds stimulated to see God's Word in new and fresh ways.

Both aspects play a crucial role in true spirituality, but they must always walk arm in arm, as necessary complements to each other. Together they bring both light and heat to the believer's life, as Jonathan Edwards understood:

There must be light in the understanding as well as fervency of heart, for if a heart has heat without light, there can be nothing divine or heavenly in that heart. On the other hand, where there is light without heat, such as a head stored with notions and speculations but having a cold and unaffected heart, there can be nothing divine in that light either.[8]

H. C. G. Moule gives us a double warning about theology and devotion:

Beware of an untheological devotion. There is no contradiction between mind and heart, between theology and devotion. Devotional hours do not mean hours when thought is absent; on the contrary, if devotion is to be real it should be characterized by thought. Meditation is not abstraction, nor is devotion dreaminess. "Thou shalt love the Lord thy God with all thy...mind" is an essential part of "the first and great commandment" (Matthew 22:37-38). A piety that is mere pietism, evangelicalism that does not continually ponder the profound truths of the New Testament, can never be strong or do any true service to the gospel cause. We must indeed beware of "untheological devotion."

But we must also beware of "undevotional theology." This is the opposite error, and it constitutes an equally grave danger. A hard, dry, intellectual study of theology will yield no spiritual fruit...it is the heart that makes the theologian; and a theology that does not spring from spiritual experience is doomed to decay, to deadness, and to disaster.[9]

Believers with deep roots refuse to settle for only what they already know of God's beauty. Like Moses, their heart cry to the Lord is "Please, show me Your glory" (Exodus 33:18). They want to see new vistas, taste sweeter waters, possess more land, and press on to greater heights. At the same time, they want to grow deeper and deeper in their knowledge and understanding of God's Word. They recognize that man is commanded to live by "every word" (Matthew 4:4) proceeding from God's mouth, and they want that Word dwelling richly in their hearts (see Colossians 3:16).

An elderly, godly pastor in Southern California was once invited to a party where a number of celebrities were also in attendance. Among them was an actor whose deep, rich voice the minister had admired for years. Summoning up his courage, he approached the actor and asked if he would mind reciting the Twenty-third Psalm, if he knew it. The actor gladly agreed, but only if this minister would do the same. The minister agreed, though a little perplexed by the attached condition.

The actor stood before the guests and in his strong, delightful voice recited this psalm he had learned as a child. It was followed by the crowd's loud applause. The actor then summoned the minister to recite. In a dry, gravely voice, the minister uttered the words, "The Lord is my shepherd…"

When he finished the psalm there was no applause—only hushed silence.

The actor then stepped forward and said to the guests, "Why do you think it is that when I recited the psalm, you applauded; yet when he recited it you were quiet?" No one had an answer. He replied, "I'll tell you why. You see, I know the psalm, but he knows the Shepherd."

Men and women with deep roots know the psalm, and the Scriptures for that matter. But above all else they know the Shepherd who lurks behind the psalm and gives life to the Scriptures. They're both worshipers and learners.

David Brainerd was a fairly obscure figure during his life as a missionary to Indians in colonial America, but the journals he left behind have had a tremendous influence in church and missions history since then. In explaining the secret of that influence, Dr. A. J. Gordon drew special attention to Brainerd's roots—his extended seasons alone with God in the New England forests:

> The hidden life, a life whose days are spent in communion with God in trying to reach the Source of power, is the life that moves the world. There may be no one to speak a eulogy over them when they are dead; and the great world may take no account of them; but by-and-by, the great moving current of these lives will begin to tell, as in the case of this young man. Indeed, the "hidden life" is crucial for becoming a spiritually felt life.[10]

SUPERNATURAL FRUIT

The second key area for the display of Christlikeness is that of supernatural fruit. We find this in the metaphor of the tree—"nor will [it] cease from yielding fruit" (Jeremiah 17:8). Most of all we find it in the life of our Lord. Luke records Christ's life as one "mighty in deed and word before God and all the people" (Luke 24:19). His short time on earth was so wildly fruitful that John records, "And there are also many other things that Jesus did, which if they were written one by one, I suppose that even the world itself could not contain the books that would be written" (John 21:25).

The inevitable result of genuinely deep roots is the presence of supernatural fruit. Jesus couldn't put it more forcefully: "He who abides in Me, and I in Him, bears much fruit; for without Me you can do nothing" (John 15:5). Notice that He doesn't say we *might* bear much fruit or that we'll bear fruit sometime in the future. If we're genuinely abiding in Him, then right now, right where we are, right who we're around, there'll be the presence of "much fruit."

What does Jesus mean by "fruit"? In Scripture, this word signifies several different aspects of spirituality:

- godly character (Galatians 5:22; Philippians 1:11; Hebrews 12:11)
- good works (Matthew 7:16-17; Luke 3:8; Colossians 1:10)
- converts (John 4:36; Colossians 1:6)
- worship (Hebrews 13:15)
- giving (2 Corinthians 9:10)

This list isn't exclusive. Fruit is anything that represents the tangible outflowing of the indwelling Christ. It's His life spilling out forcefully through us before God, others, and the world.

Such supernatural fruit is *divinely produced.* It is God-originated, God-energized, God-produced. In the Christian life we're never called to be manufacturers of godly living, only distributors. Paul prayed that we might be "filled with the fruits of righteousness which are *by* Jesus Christ to the glory and praise of God" (Philippians 1:11). And he said that "the fruit *of the Spirit* is love" (Galatians 5:22).

Remember, handiwork worthy of the name of God can only be produced by God. If He's to be glorified in our lives, it will require stepping aside so Christ can move forward unhindered, since He states so strongly, "Without Me you can do nothing" (John 15:5). This is the heartbeat of New Covenant living and ministry. It's the bringing forth of fruit not our own, for a glory not our own, by a power not our own.

Supernatural fruit is also *humanly surprising.* The ultimate purpose of our fruit bearing is to glorify God. "By this My Father is glorified, that you bear much fruit" (John 15:8). And central to glorifying God is the element of surprise.

One of the repeated responses to Jesus' life was that of astonishment. "The people were astonished at His teaching" (Matthew 7:28). "So all...marveled" (Luke 4:22). "And they were greatly amazed in themselves beyond measure, and marveled" (Mark 6:51). The Gospels are replete with statements like these describing the people's startled reactions to the life and ministry of Christ. Whatever else might be said about the life of Christ, one thing is for sure: It was inescapably surprising.

The Flavor of Adventure

John Wesley was once asked the secret to the fast growth of Methodism. One might have expected him to talk about evangelism or organizational skills or outreach to the needy. Instead, he replied, "Our people die well." The Methodist believers approached their last days on this earth with a peace and joy that defied reason, and their surprising example preached louder than any sermon or tract.

What about us? Do we allow Christ the freedom to relive His surprising life through us, or have we bound that irrepressible life with chains of religious respectability? If you know Christ, I'm certain there rises up within you an utter discontent with predictable piety, safe spirituality, and dull, drab rule keeping. You want something far more, something that sings, something that soars, something that brings surprise and adventure to your life.

That something is the life of Christ seeking to burst through you. Why not go ahead and let Him have His way? If you do, I'll promise you one thing: It will remove the word *boring* from your existence.

The Taste of God Working Through You

What does surprising Christianity look like?

To help you explore this on your own, let me suggest that you go through the Sermon on the Mount in Matthew 5–7 and highlight all the places where Christ is calling us to a surprising way of living. Then read the book of James for a great follow-up. Finally, ask the Lord to show you specific ways He wants to surprise others through you.

Several months ago I was pulled over for speeding. I would like to be able to say there was some justifiable reason for why I was going over the speed limit, but the reality was I just wasn't paying attention.

It's bad enough to be given a speeding ticket, but even worse when you're a pastor. The most uncomfortable part is when the officer asks, "What is your occupation?"

"Well, actually I'm a pastor. I teach people about Romans 13 and how they should obey the laws of the land." (I've never actually tried saying that, but I've certainly thought about it.)

As the policeman wrote up the ticket that day, I couldn't shake a strong sense of the Lord prompting me to speak words of gratitude to this officer. After he'd given me the ticket, I said, "Sir, I just want to thank you as a citizen for the work you and your fellow officers do for our community. I've served on a grand jury twice now, and I had no idea of the things you guys go through, the dangers you face, and the pressures you endure. I just wanted to say thanks for the great job you do in helping to keep our community safe."

He still gave me the ticket (part of me was hoping God would reward His servant for following through on His prompting). But he looked at me with the most stunned expression and finally said, "Thanks so much. I've never had anyone tell me that before. You're the easiest ticket I've ever given."

Now, I have no idea whether the officer was impacted by my words. But when my teenage son noticed my ticket and was reading it with great delight, he said, "Hey, Dad, I go to school with this officer's son. He's told me that his dad is really turned off to religion." I've prayed that those words the Lord gave me might soften his heart. But whether they do or not, there was still that clean joy for me of having tasted God doing something through me I would never have thought of doing on my own. I've also prayed that God would help me taste the clean joy of driving within the speed limits from now on!

SPREADING BRANCHES

We find now the final image of branches that push forward with their arms of luxuriant fruit. God says of repentant Israel, "His branches shall spread [literally, 'walk']" (Hosea 14:6). This too mirrors the life of our Lord who came first to His own people but reached out to the whole world as well. When His disciples sought to localize Him and get Him to settle down to minister in just one place, He responded, "Let us go into the next towns, that I may preach there also, because for this purpose I have come forth" (Mark 1:38). Christ's branches were ever reaching out, seeking to shelter and nourish all those with ears to hear.

In what direction should our branches be extending? The same as for our Lord—toward two primary groups, believers and unbelievers.

According to Christ's priority in John 15, our next calling after abiding in Him (John 15:1-11) is to love our fellow believers (John 15:12-17). As we're genuinely abiding in Christ, His life will propel us toward significant and supernatural loving of other Christians. We'll be like the Thessalonians whom Paul commended: "But concerning brotherly love you have no need that I should write to you, for you yourselves are taught by God to love one another" (1 Thessalonians 4:9).

The rivers of living waters within us are pushing forward to unite with the rivers of living waters within other believers. Our love of the brethren is ultimately a gifted love, a Spirit-engendered love that reaches out to other believers, not because they're worthy, but because they house the presence of God within them.

Love so unexplainable among the early Christians had a striking impact on those around them. One pagan emperor noted, "These Christians love one another before they're even acquainted."

If our new nature is to have its longings for dispensing God-stained love satisfied, one of the things that must happen is for our branches to be vitally connected with those of other believers as part of the great forest of God, which exists to bring glory to Him.

Our branches aren't to remain entwined only with other believers, but to lengthen out literally to the ends of the earth. "You shall receive power when the Holy Spirit has come upon you; and you shall be witnesses to me in Jerusalem, and in all Judea and Samaria, and to the end of the earth" (Acts 1:8).

Scotland's George MacLeod expressed our mission this way:

> I simply argue that the cross should be raised at the center of the marketplace as well as on the steeple of the church. I am recovering the claim that Jesus was not crucified in a cathedral between two candles, but on a cross between two thieves; on the town's garbage heap; at a crossroad, so cosmopolitan they had to write His title in Hebrew and Latin and Greek...at the kind of a place where cynics talk smut, and thieves curse, and soldiers gamble. Because that is where He died. And that is what He died for. And that is what He died about. That is where church-men ought to be and what church-men ought to be about.[11]

As you read that declaration, did you find something stirring within you, saying "yes" to the adventure of following Christ into the real world to meet sinners on their turf and tell them of a God they never knew existed? That stirring, that "yes" (though it may be faint) is the redemptive restlessness of the Holy Spirit within you.

Henry Martyn wrote, "The Spirit of Christ is the spirit of missions and the nearer we get to Him the more intensely missionary we must become."[12] The life of Christ within us is restless while there are still lost people wandering about in spiritual blindness and sin. "For the Son of Man has come to seek and to save that which was lost" (Luke 19:10).

God doesn't call us to do evangelism and witnessing *for* Him, but rather *with* Him. He's on the move, actively seeking lost sheep, lost coins, and lost sons (see Luke 15). This is the heart of God. We don't need to cultivate a heart for the lost; we were given a fully cultivated one at conversion. What we need to do is stop feeling guilty that we can't squeeze concern for the lost from our old heart (which will never happen anyway) and flee to that part of us that already cares deeply about their plight. It's called our "new heart" (Ezekiel 36:26), the place where the greatest missionary of all time dwells—Jesus Christ. His passion for the lost is just as real, just as intact as it was two thousand years ago. It simply awaits release.

Unfortunately, surveys have shown that after a person has begun growing as a Christian for two years, they no longer have even one significant non-Christian friend. How contrary this is to the life of Christ within us who was known as a "friend of tax collectors and sinners." An inevitable part of the life of Christ flowing out through us will be fishing for men and seeking the lost. This will be done by life and by word, but all of it must be done through Christ if it is to have the touch of God upon it.

Four Questions

I've found that these three images of deep roots, supernatural fruit, and long branches are extremely helpful in knowing what to aim for in seeking to supernaturally influence others. As I'm involved in another believer's life, I ask four questions:

How are their roots? Are they personally going deeper into God than before? Are they balanced in their pursuit, growing as worshipers and learners?

How is their fruit? Are they deepening in their dependence? In what ways are they living surprising lives?

How are their branches? Are they significantly involved with other believers? Are they known for their love? Are they significantly involved with other unbelievers? Are they growing in their witness of Christ, both here and abroad?

Most of all, are these things maturing in our own lives? With that last question in mind, I urge you to take a moment now and ask God to show you the next specific step He would have you take in light of what you've read in this chapter.

Keeping Second Things Second

The art of being wise is the art
of knowing what to overlook.

WILLIAM JAMES

I read several years ago about a pastor who woke early one Sunday morning to find that all the roads out of his neighborhood were impassible due to heavy snow. The only way he could get to his church was to skate along the frozen river that ran past his house toward the church.

After skating to the church, he was putting away his skates when one of the elders spotted him. "You don't mean to tell me you were skating on the Lord's day!" he exclaimed. A meeting of all the elders was promptly called to discuss the situation.

When the pastor explained to them that the only possible way he could get to the church that morning was by skating, they realized he had a good point. Still, it was skating on the Lord's day.

Finally, one elder asked the pastor, "Well, did you enjoy it?"

When the pastor answered no, the whole matter was dropped.

I hope that story is fictional, but I wouldn't be surprised in the least if such a thing actually happened. The church today, as throughout history, is characterized far too often by what one writer calls "an obsession with the insignificant." It's losing sight of the main thing and thus majoring on the minor and minoring on the major.

It's what causes churches to split over the color of the carpet in the sanctuary, the style of cross over the pulpit, the kind of music and instruments in the worship, the translation of the Bible read, the use of makeup for women, the kind of schooling for children, the degree of political involvement, and on and on. Worst of all, it badly blurs and even obscures the supernatural beauty God has created the church to display. As Joe Aldrich puts it,

> Our world is full of professing Christians who claim to believe the truth but are producing ugliness. They can't get along. They fight, gossip, and often act as if they were weaned on dill pickles.[1]

Clearly this isn't what the rivers of living water within us were meant to produce. How then can we sidestep the temptation to get hung up on secondary issues and have no room left over to get hung up on what is primary? How do we keep second things second?

Earlier I noted that our goal in spiritually influencing others is to cooperate with God in helping them fulfill their whole potential in Christ. In pursuing it, we must be sensitive to the Spirit in knowing where and how to challenge or confront; we need divine wisdom to know where and how to strengthen and nourish; and we need grace to know what things to just leave alone.

Herein lies one of the greatest challenges in influencing others toward their whole potential in Christ. When is the time to confront someone about something, and when is the time to just leave it alone? Over the centuries untold harm has been done to the name of Christ because of confusion in these issues. We'll look closely at them now.

You may find this chapter refreshing. Or you may find it puzzling and be drawn to the Scriptures to see if the things I say here are really true. Or perhaps you'll be bothered, even enough to give up on reading any more of the book. When this chapter was still in manuscript form, I let several different individuals and groups read and review it, and I received each of those responses.

All I can do is encourage you to be like the Bereans in Acts 17:10-11. Search the Scriptures for yourself to see whether these things are true; hold on to the wheat, and blow away the chaff.

One thing I tell my congregation is "Know for sure that at the judgment seat of Christ, there's one thing our Lord will never ask you: 'What did Dwight believe?'" We must all come to our own convictions and opinions of what Scripture is teaching from our own studying of the text, not from anyone else, nor from the propensity of our flesh to simply follow the majority rule. Too often we look around to see what others are doing on an issue rather than wrestling before God to see what He would have us do. To help you in the wrestling, I want to introduce you to new ways of thinking on this topic.

ESSENTIALS VERSUS NONESSENTIALS

Probably you've seen or heard the slogan, "The main thing is to keep the main thing the main thing." This is fantastic advice for becoming a person of supernatural influence. But I would also add this, "The second thing is to keep second things second." Indeed, it isn't possible to keep the main thing main if we aren't careful to keep the second things second.

The seventeenth-century theologian Rupert Meldenius is credited with the maxim, "In essentials, unity; in nonessentials, liberty; in all things, charity." I don't know if it can be put better than that. Certain essential doctrines and practices must not be deviated from in any way if a body of believers is to be considered historic, orthodox Christians. These essentials include:

- the inerrancy of Scripture
- the deity and virgin birth of Christ
- the substitutionary atonement of Christ

- the bodily resurrection of Christ
- the personal return of Christ

These are *essentials,* absolutely foundational to historic, orthodox Christianity, and on such issues there must be uncompromised unity.

Yet any body of believers will encounter far more issues that are nonessentials, areas where Scripture hasn't given a specific command. These are often called "neutral issues." Paul addresses them in Romans 14 and in 1 Corinthians 8 and 10. In these areas, we're to practice responsible liberty.

The crucial factor in dealing with the nonessentials is to maintain an atmosphere of love and respect among believers. According to Paul, believers can come to the opposite conclusion before God on these issues and both be right at the same time: "For one believes he may eat all things, but he who is weak eats only vegetables. Let not him who eats despise him who does not eat, and let not him who does not eat judge him who eats; for God has received him" (Romans 14:2-3). Rather than telling the Roman believers whether they could eat meat or only vegetables, he gave guidelines on how every believer is to go before the Lord to gain a personal conviction on the matter from Him. This is quite different from what Paul had to say earlier in this letter about justification by faith alone—an issue God had settled once and for all.

Paul was saying that on nonessential issues we must come to our own conviction before the Lord as to what we should do. Equally important, we must not require other believers to share our conviction. Rather, we're to respect the fact that they've heard from God as clearly as we have. Their leading is just different.

If I could wish one thing upon the body of Christ today, it would be this: to warmly and respectfully give one another freedom in nonessential areas. That would revolutionize our life within the church as well as our testimony to the outside.

But how do we discern the essential from the nonessential? This is no small matter, for failure to do so can bring tragic results. When neutral things are made essential, you end up with legalism. Hard, stiff, judgmental churchianity. But when essential issues are made neutral you end up with apostasy—insipid, anything-goes, man-constructed religiosity. Spiritual discernment is required if we're to be, as Christ was, full of both grace (not making neutral things essential) and truth (not making essential things neutral).

I believe the starting point for this crucial endeavor is the ability to discern between what is genuinely, unmistakably *biblical* versus that which is only *cultural, traditional,* or *personal.*

Christian researchers estimate that in any given culture about 70 to 80 percent of Christian practice ultimately falls under the categories of what is cultural, traditional, or personal. I have no doubt that they're correct. As Erwin Lutzer notes, "We are locked into our own culture much more than we realize. Yet we always want to absolutize our personal preferences."[2]

Just think through our standard worship service. How much of it is unmistakably biblical? And how much, when you get down to it, is really just cultural, personal, or traditional? In which of those four categories would you place each of the following?
- gathering for worship on Sunday
- gathering for worship on Sunday morning
- holding Sunday-school classes
- accompanying our singing with piano or organ
- accompanying our singing with guitar or drums
- standing up during the service to "greet those around you"
- passing the offering plate
- having an altar call
- communicating the Word of God

I think you get the picture. Communicating God's Word is the only item on this list that I believe the Bible clearly mandates. All the others fall into the other categories of cultural, personal, or traditional. And yet a huge portion of the disarray in the church today is directly linked to our inability or unwillingness to distinguish between these four categories. Church splits rarely occur over issues that are clearly defined biblically.

Moreover, when we make second things first, the testimony of Christ Himself is damaged. As Charles Spurgeon expressed it, we start to see Him as the moral bill collector of the universe instead of as the unrivaled Lover of our souls.

How should we understand each of these categories—biblical, cultural, traditional, personal—and how are they different from one another?

The Biblical

The biblical category includes what is clearly and unmistakably revealed or mandated in the Scriptures and is in keeping with the New Covenant. Whatever is addressed in the New Testament falls into this category, assuming the proper contextual, historical, linguistic interpretation. Whatever is revealed or mandated in the Old Testament with New Testament confirmation would also fall into this category. Admittedly, making such a determination can be difficult and confusing at times, but it's a critical exercise, lest we go back under the Law, which Christ died to set us free from.

Stealing, for example, is clearly wrong. It's condemned by the Old Covenant (Deuteronomy 5:19) and also in the New Covenant (Ephesians 4:28). What about giving? It's clearly commanded in the Old Covenant, where it was mandated as one-tenth of one's income (along with other offerings). Does this continue in the New Covenant? Yes, but the percentage is changed. The percentage of our giving under the New Covenant is "So let each one give *as he purposes in his heart*" (2 Corinthians 9:7). The strict 10 percent is altered in the New Covenant to whatever percentage a person can give joyously, sacrificially, and without grudging.

Or let's take the eating of pork. This was clearly forbidden in the Old

Covenant (Leviticus 11:7), yet the prohibition is completely lifted in the New (Acts 10:15). God's people are completely free to eat ham sandwiches if they so choose.

As we think through the appropriateness of any Old Covenant command in our lives today, we should ask these questions:

Is this a command or principle that continues unaltered by the New Covenant? Most of the Ten Commandments fall into this category.

Is this a command or principle that continues but is altered by the New Covenant? For instance, the law of love is upgraded from loving others as we love ourselves (Leviticus 19:18) to loving one another as Christ has loved us (John 13:34; 15:12). Adultery is expanded to the inside of the heart (Matthew 5:27-28) and not just the physical act (Deuteronomy 5:18).

Is this a command or principle that is abrogated by the New Covenant? Things like the eating of certain foods, circumcision, or the observance of religious feasts (Acts 10:14-15; 15:1-29; Colossians 2:16) would fall under this category.

Is this something in the New Covenant that is prescriptive or descriptive? Is this something that happened and should always continue to happen (prescriptive), or is this something that just happened with no indication that it should continue (descriptive)? This distinction is crucial for interpreting the book of Acts, which every fringe group tends to camp on for validation of their practices. Acts is, for the most part, a description of the first forty years of the church, not a prescription for how it should always be. In Acts, Gentile believers are commanded to abstain from foods offered to idols (Acts 15: 20), but in Corinth eating food offered to idols is a neutral issue (1 Corinthians 8:4-13).

As I said, these issues are crucial if we're not to go back under the yoke of Law or turn grace into an excuse for loose living.

We must also recognize that not all teaching is equally clear in the Bible or to be held with the same degree of conviction. Peter wrote that

Paul's epistles contained "some things hard to understand" (2 Peter 3:16). What an encouraging verse—even the apostle Peter had difficulty grasping some of Paul's passages. How many of us are ready to echo a hearty amen to that! (And Paul might well have said the same about some things in Peter's epistles.)

We must be careful to emphasize forcefully what Scripture emphasizes forcefully and to hold with a looser grip those things that simply aren't as certain.

For instance, I wouldn't insist on many of the details of the Lord's return (as I understand them) with the same certainty I have about the deity of Christ. My convictions on speaking in tongues aren't as strong as my convictions about salvation by faith alone.

I like to assess such issues using three criteria. If I were a betting man, wagering that my position on a particular issue is right, (1) what would I be willing to lose lunch for? (2) what would I be willing to lose my house for? and (3) what would I be willing to lose my life for?

I'm willing to lose my life for a small number of absolute, unquestionable essentials—the deity of Christ, for example, or salvation by faith alone. Less clear but more numerous are the issues I would be willing to lose my house for, such as a premillennial view of the end times and local church government by a plurality of elders. Far more numerous are the issues I'm willing to lose lunch over, where my thoughts are more opinions than convictions—such as identifying the "sons of God" mentioned in Genesis 6 or the question of whether Jesus descended into hell after He was buried.

We do a grave disservice to ourselves and others if we hold all biblical teachings with equal conviction. Peter didn't say that all of Paul's writings were hard to understand, but some unquestionably were. The virgin birth of Christ and properly interpreting the "husband of one wife" requirement for elders simply aren't on the same plane of certainty. We must be careful to separate our opinions from our convictions.

Moreover, not all biblical values are equally weighty. Christ made that unmistakably clear when He said, "Woe to you, scribes and Pharisees, hypocrites! For you pay tithe of mint and anise and cumin, and have neglected *the weightier matters* of the law: justice and mercy and faith" (Matthew 23:23). We must give greatest weight to those issues and values that God gives greatest weight to, lest we major on minors and minor on majors. "For I desire mercy and not sacrifice," the Lord tells us, "and the knowledge of God more than burnt offerings" (Hosea 6:6).

The Cultural

Beliefs, values, and practices that are part of a shared community fall into the category of "cultural." Culture has been defined as "the patterned way in which people do things together." The church has its own culture just as much as society does. Far more than we realize, much of what happens in our churches is determined more by the culture we live in than by the Bible itself.

The contemporary Christian music of our day is a good example of this. There's nothing biblical or unbiblical about the music itself (that is, the instruments used and the notes that are played); it's simply in keeping with much of the music in our culture. If you go to a church in Nigeria or Indonesia, you'll find their praise music very different from ours and also from each other's.

There's actually no such thing as Christian music. Nowhere in your Bible will you find an inspired melody or chord or tempo. You'll search in vain to see whether God prefers hymns sung with drums and guitar, with the organ, or a cappella. The lyrics are what make a song "Christian" or not. We're to worship "in truth" (John 4:24), and thus the words of the song are the crucial issue, not the music itself. Both contemporary praise songs and the hymns of old have some lyrics that are thoroughly biblical as well as some that are frankly heretical. The music itself is neutral, hard as that is for some believers to accept. And historically the music that accompanies the lyrics has almost always been drawn from the culture of the day. Some of our great hymns were even set to the music of the taverns and music halls of their time.

The important issue here isn't to despise what is cultural, but to be able to discern between it and the biblical, and to be willing to live counter-culturally when Christlikeness requires.

THE TRADITIONAL

The traditional category involves beliefs, values, and practices that come as a result of what has been done in the past. This isn't necessarily bad, for many wonderful traditions rest on solid, biblical grounding. The grave danger comes when the traditional and biblical collide. This is what Christ was addressing when He said, "Thus you have made the commandment of God of no effect by your tradition.... And in vain they worship Me, teaching as doctrines the commandments of men" (Matthew 15:6-9).

So much of our Christianity and church practices are set in place because of tradition. The time, the order, and the length of the services are almost always the result of tradition. Again, this isn't necessarily bad, and it's important that we as God's children recognize and appreciate the good and godly portions of our spiritual heritage. "Look to the rock from which you were hewn, and to the hole of the pit from which you were dug. Look to Abraham your father, and to Sarah who bore you" (Isaiah 51:1-2).

But the danger comes when *the tradition runs contrary to the Word of God.* "Beware lest anyone cheat you through philosophy and empty deceit, according to the tradition of men, according to the basic principles of the world, and not according to Christ" (Colossians 2:8). Reasonable, good-sounding traditions continue to be accepted even when they run contrary to Christ and the Scriptures.

Danger also comes when *the tradition is viewed as the Word of God;*

that is, "teaching as doctrines the commandments of men" (Matthew 15:9). I continue to be amazed at the number of people I run into who genuinely believe Jesus used the *King James Version,* or else that Paul wrote it. The King James has a wonderful tradition, but it is *not* God's authorized version. Yet I've heard preachers say that the King James is the only trustworthy version and the one God intended man to read (which is a real bummer for those born before 1611).

In addition, danger arises when *the tradition thwarts a fresh move of the Spirit.* "No one puts new wine into old wineskins.… New wine must be put into new wineskins" (Mark 2:22). The tombstone for many churches is engraved with the words, "We've never done it that way before."

Every fresh movement of God's Spirit in history has wreaked havoc with the church traditions of that day. In every case there has been a change in the music and songs used for worship, not unlike what we're seeing today. Those who are willing to be carried along in the new direction of God's Spirit taste the rich wine of knowing Him and being used by Him in powerful new ways. Those who are unwilling to take the risk of letting go of what worked in the past consign themselves to the dullness and deadness of old-wineskin living.

God never asks us to give up what is genuinely biblical, but He requires that we hold the traditional with a loose grip so He can replace it when He wants.

THE PERSONAL

The fourth category involves beliefs, values, and practices that are the result of personal convictions or opinions. These convictions and opinions often are informed by one's understanding of Scripture, but they're recognized to be not binding on others. We find this most clearly in Romans 14:1-23, where we find important principles to keep in mind.

Distinguishing the Fence from the Tree

First, *these are issues in which the Scriptures provide latitude.* In other words, they aren't specifically mandated by the Word of God. The areas Paul chooses here are kinds of foods to eat (Romans 14:2), day of worship (14:5-6), drinking of wine (14:21). We have freedom within each of these areas, and our calling is to follow our conscience before God (14:5,22-23).

We do not have freedom, however, to break the clearly revealed will of God. We're free to drink wine but not to get drunk (Ephesians 5:18). We're free to eat food offered to idols (1 Corinthians 8:4-6) but never to commit idolatry (10:7).

The first case of legalism in the Bible is found in Genesis 2 and 3. God gave a specific command to Adam: "Of every tree of the garden you may freely eat; but of the tree of the knowledge of good and evil you shall not eat, for in the day that you eat of it you shall surely die" (2:16-17). There's no latitude here; it's not a neutral issue, but the clearly revealed Word of God—an essential.

But later, when the serpent tempts Eve, note carefully her response: "Of the fruit of the tree which is in the midst of the garden, God has said, 'You shall not eat it, nor shall you touch it, lest you die'" (Genesis 3:3). Did God ever tell Adam and Eve they couldn't touch the tree? No.

Was Eve wrong to make the personal choice to never touch the tree? Absolutely not. In fact, not touching is a great way to keep from eating; works every time. She had complete freedom never to go near that tree. Where was she wrong? To make not touching the tree into the command of God and to place it on equal footing with His command not to eat. I like to think of her conviction not to touch the tree as "the fence." It was a personal choice to stay farther away from the tree than God had specifically mandated.

Using this picture, we can think of any essential issue as "the tree" and nonessential or neutral issues as "the fence."

The great problem with legalism is three-fold:
- failure to distinguish the fence from the tree
- promoting the fence *as* the tree
- judging others who don't see the situation the same way we do

Take for instance the issue of drinking alcohol. What is the tree? "Do not be drunk" (Ephesians 5:18). There isn't an iota of legalism in that command; it's the clear, unmistakable will of God. Now, does that mean Scripture prohibits any drinking of alcohol? Clearly not (see 1 Timothy 5:23 or Matthew 11:19). Are believers free to totally abstain from drinking? Absolutely, and many wisely choose to do so.

But what believers are not free to do is to claim that God views drinking as being equal to drunkenness. Drunkenness is the tree; abstaining from drink is the fence. One is essential (avoiding drunkenness), the other neutral.

In looking at these personal issues, the starting point is to distinguish the fence from the tree, the biblical from the neutral.

Sensitivity to Conscience

A second principle from Romans 14 is that *all believers must be true to their own conscience before God.* Just because you know in your mind that you're free to do something doesn't necessarily mean you should do it. If, for whatever reason, your conscience is signaling reservations about going ahead with the issue, stop in your tracks. Don't move forward until your conscience is able to give you the green light, regardless of your theological understanding of freedom.

Paul said, "Let each be fully convinced in his own mind" (Romans 14:5). "Do you have faith? Have it to yourself before God. Happy is he who does not condemn himself in what he approves. But he who doubts is condemned if he eats, because he does not eat from faith; for whatever is not from faith is sin" (Romans 14:22-23).

Walking in Love

A third principle from Romans is this: *Be willing to limit your freedom for the sake of the genuinely weaker brother and his conscience.* Here's the difference between adolescent freedom in the Lord and mature freedom in the Lord. Adolescent freedom is preoccupied with enjoying its liberty and proving that liberty to those around. Mature freedom recognizes that the use of one's liberty in a particular area might cause another believer to trip or stumble in their own walk with God.

Paul wrote, "It is good neither to eat meat nor drink wine nor do anything by which your brother stumbles or is offended or is made weak" (Romans 14:21). The mature believer realizes that he or she is not only free from the law but also free for love.

This restriction of our freedom is appropriate toward genuinely weaker brothers, but not everyone who might object to your actions will fall in that category. In *Lifestyle Evangelism,* Joe Aldrich makes a distinction between the genuinely weaker brother and the "professional" weaker brother.[3] The professional is the Pharisee, the hardened legalist whom neither Jesus nor Paul ever accommodated. In regard to those individuals, God commands: "Stand fast therefore in the liberty by which Christ has made us free, and do not be entangled again with a yoke of bondage" (Galatians 5:1).

Respecting the Fences of Others

A final major principle from Romans 14: *Develop your own convictions, but stop your judging.* Wrestle through these neutral issues before God, and gain what you believe to be His mind on them. "One person esteems one day above another; another esteems every day alike. Let each be fully convinced in his own mind" (Romans 14:5).

Recognize that you're dealing with a fence, not the tree. And God has given others the freedom to build different fences. "Let not him who eats despise him who does not eat, and let not him who does not eat judge him who eats; for God has received him. Who are you to judge another's servant? To his own master he stands or falls. Indeed…God is able to make him stand" (14:3-4).

Note the two things we're to avoid concerning others' fences: judging and despising. One is external, the other internal. We're not to point out and speak badly (judging) of others' conclusions on a neutral issue. But neither are we to internally dismiss and write off as unspiritual (despise) the person who has a different sort of fence.

Putting the Principles into Practice

So we've looked at the difference between what is genuinely biblical versus cultural, traditional, or personal. Now let's see where the rubber meets the road. Think about each item on the following list. Is it an essential issue or a neutral issue? Go ahead and note your thoughts by jotting a letter in front of each item, indicating into which category you would place it—biblical (B), cultural (C), traditional (T), or personal (P):

___ praying before meals
___ having a daily devotional time
___ having a daily devotional time in the morning
___ going to church each Sunday
___ lifting hands during worship
___ dancing during worship
___ allowing children to run inside a church building
___ discipling instruction in group settings
___ discipling instruction one-on-one
___ playing golf on Sunday morning

___ drinking alcohol
___ drinking alcohol in public
___ dancing
___ kissing before marriage
___ having sex before marriage
___ having an abortion
___ using birth control
___ masturbating
___ driving the speed limit
___ lying in a job interview
___ lying on a tax return
___ schooling choices for our children

___ owning a luxury car

___ watching R-rated movies

___ listening to rock music

___ having cable television

___ gambling

___ playing the lottery

___ wearing long hair (men)

___ wearing short hair (women)

___ piercing your body

___ tattooing your body

___ wearing earrings (men)

___ wearing name-brand clothes

___ wearing expensive clothes

___ smoking tobacco

___ taking medication for depression

___ taking marijuana for medicinal use

___ bartending

___ working sixty or more hours per week

___ working outside the home (women)

___ giving money to secular causes

___ dating and marrying of mixed races

___ aligning with a particular political party

I hope you're seeing that this is no simple or easy exercise. It stretches all of us, regardless of our backgrounds and preferences.

Let me conclude this chapter by giving you three reasons this ability to distinguish the essential from the nonessential is so vital.

We're Not All Called to the Same Role

The first reason is that the expression of Christlikeness can vary dramatically from individual to individual. Depending upon our gifts, our calling, our personality, and our background, there can be tremendous diversity in how godliness is exhibited. No better example of this can be given than the contrast between Jesus and John the Baptist. "For John came neither eating nor drinking, and they say, 'He has a demon.' The Son of Man came eating and drinking, and they say, 'Look, a glutton and a wine-bibber, a friend of tax collectors and sinners!'" (Matthew 11:18-19).

John came with an austere, somewhat ascetic lifestyle. Honey and locust were his cuisine, and little more than a loincloth served as his clothing. How did Jesus view John's spirituality? A legalist or ascetic? No, in fact

He said, "Assuredly, I say to you, among those born of women there has not risen one greater than John the Baptist" (Matthew 11:11). Jesus came with a more robust, able-to-enjoy-life approach. What did John say of Him? "He's a hedonist and needs to rein in His enjoyment of life"? Of course not. What he said was that he wasn't worthy to loose His sandal strap (see John 1:27). Two very different approaches to neutral issues, but likeminded on the essential—the kingdom of God.

This is so critical for the body of Christ. So many of our differences really center on neutral issues, yet instead of being able to celebrate and bless these differences, we judge and withdraw. If I'm really committed to seeing other believers become like Jesus, then I must be preeminently concerned about what Christlikeness looks like for them before God.

I have a good friend in our church who was saved out of the drug culture of California and has many biker friends to this day. He has a few tattoos on his body, some with Scriptures and spiritual sayings. He can't talk about what Christ has done for him without being brought to tears. He leads other bikers to the Lord on a fairly consistent basis, for he's able to connect with them right where they are. I could never do what he does, but I love to sit back and watch God use this godly man in amazing ways.

His Christlikeness looks very different from that of another friend of mine in our church, a three-star general in the U.S. Army. He's able to have spiritual influence on other soldiers and officers in ways neither I nor my biker friend ever could. These two men couldn't be further apart in terms of their backgrounds, vocation, and personalities. Yet they're identical in terms of what matters most—their abandonment to glorifying Christ through their daily lives.

In spiritually influencing others, we must delight in seeing the uniqueness of their God-crafted niche and help them max out in the design God has for them. Far too much discipleship and mentoring today is a pressured attempt to reproduce God's design for the discipler in the life of the disciplee. God has placed within the body of Christ marvelous diversity, and He intends this diversity to blossom as each individual plays his own part through the Spirit. Doing this is impossible unless we can distinguish essentials from nonessentials.

God Wants Us to Listen for His Voice Alone

A second reason for distinguishing the essential from the nonessential is to help other believers hear the voice of God for themselves on neutral issues.

One of the most important aspects of spiritually influencing others is helping them wrestle through these neutral issues *for themselves* before the Lord. Too often in the church we're allowing people to escape their calling to go personally before God on these issues; instead, we make the decisions for them. We do it to keep things safe and prevent less mature believers from misusing their freedom. But in doing so we rob them of one of the most critical aspects of supernatural living: hearing the voice of God for themselves.

I find it interesting that in Romans 14 Paul never said who was right or wrong on the issues mentioned there. Nor did he take a side on them. He simply offered guidelines to help those believers wrestle for themselves about what God would have them to do. That's the role we're to play as well.

We Don't Need to Get Hung Up on Nonessentials

A third reason for separating the essential from the nonessential is this: When we get hung up on the wrong things, there's no room left over to get hung up on the right things. Paul said, "For the kingdom of God is not eating and drinking, but righteousness and peace and joy in the Holy Spirit" (Romans 14:17).

A couple of summers ago our church paid for my wife and me to take a cruise, and we had a wonderful time. On one of our first nights out, our assigned dinner partners were a nice couple about our age. We chatted for a while, then I asked what each of them did for a living.

They looked a little sheepishly at each other, then the man said, "We're professional gamblers." Obviously, this wasn't in the range of answers we were expecting. The husband, it turns out, is one of the foremost five-card stud players in the world, playing routinely with celebrities such as Michael Jordan and Jack Nicholson. He and his wife play only in places where gambling is legal, they're aboveboard in paying taxes on their earnings, and they're honest in their dealings with others.

We enjoyed getting to know this couple. God prompted me to keep pursuing them, loving them right where they were and as they were. I picked their brains on the various aspects of card gambling—how to know when someone's bluffing, when it is best to fold, and so on. I asked if they would be playing aboard the ship some evening so we could come and watch. They said no—they were on vacation!

Soon the tables turned, and they asked me the dreaded question, "So what do you do?" I don't think my answer was exactly in their range of expectations either. There was a noticeable drop in their countenances when I told them I was a pastor. I'm sure they were expecting to be preached at or at least judged by us. But my wife and I just kept talking with them, asking more about their lives and backgrounds. I got the man to share his fascinating story of growing up in Brooklyn and how he became so great at poker.

At one point I said to them, "You know, as far as I see it, what you do and what the average stockbroker does are about the same thing." The woman looked at me and said with intensity, "This guy gets it!" She had grown up in a strict, legalistic Christian home, and her parents weren't exactly thrilled with her choice of careers, to say the least.

This couple became totally relaxed around us and began asking us questions. In fact the husband, who was a Jew, asked me point-blank to tell him how I'd become a Christian and why I'd left tennis to become a preacher. It was a wonderful time sharing how Christ had touched my life and Sandy's as well.

You may or may not agree with my assessment of gambling and the stock market; the real point I want to make from our experience is that we need to be careful about what we get hung up on. We all get hung up on something. And when we get hung up on the nonessentials, the essentials have no opportunity to make a significant appearance.

So let the old saying burn its way deeply into your heart and life:

In essentials, unity.
In nonessentials, liberty.
In all things, charity.

According to His Working

In whatever man does without God,
he must fail miserably—or succeed more miserably.
GEORGE MACDONALD

D r. J. Wilbur Chapman recalls one of the most significant events in his life as the day he determined to stop working for God. It was a Monday morning, and though things were going well at church and with his ministry, his inner soul was parched and tired. Taking up a newspaper, he began reading a sermon by Dr. F. B. Meyer in which he found this interesting comment, "There are many men who have never yet learned the difference between working for God, and allowing God to work through them. That's the reason so many ministers and Christian workers break down."

Dr. Chapman wrote afterwards, "The Lord then enlightened my eyes. I'd been working my fingertips off for the Lord. It's now going to be different. Kneeling down I prayed, 'Lord from today onward, pour Thyself through me to them.'" This was the beginning of a worldwide ministry that saw thousands trust Christ.[1]

The distinction between working *for* God and working *with* Him (or perhaps better: God working through us) can't be emphasized too strongly. It's literally the difference as to whether God shows up or not in our attempts to influence others. God never calls us to undertake something He doesn't intend to do Himself. He's just looking for people who find their greatest honor in staying out of His way.

Earlier we looked at the importance of staying focused on the main thing, helping others become more like Christ in all His radical wonder. This was clearly Paul's goal: "Him we preach, warning every man and teaching every man in all wisdom, *that we may present every man perfect in Christ Jesus*" (Colossians 1:28).

Now look closely at the following verse: "To this end I also labor, *striving according to His working which works in me mightily*" (1:29). These two verses must not be separated from each other. Any striving on our part to help others become like Christ must be a dependent, Christ-energized striving before anything of divine and eternal consequence will occur.

"We are not sent to battle for God," Oswald Chambers said, "but to be used by God in His battlings."[2] God never designed us to serve others on His behalf, but to be His personal suit of clothes through whom He could serve others. He wants to touch with our hands, speak with our tongues, walk with our feet, and, most of all, love through our hearts. This is our only hope or possibility for supernatural influence.

CHRIST'S DEPENDENCE

We see this modeled perfectly in the life of our Lord. At every turn He radically depended upon the Father alone. He was utterly dependent upon His Father's *lead.* "My Father has been working until now, and I have been working" (John 5:17). Jesus didn't come to initiate a work for God; He joined in the working His Father was already doing. In the same way, our calling is not to be busy for God, but rather to "keep in step with the Spirit" (Galatians 5:25, NIV). The Spirit of God is already on the move, waiting for us to join Him in where He's headed. He has little interest in joining us down a side road we've chosen for serving God.

Christ was dependent upon His Father's *example.* "Most assuredly, I say to you, the Son can do nothing of Himself, but what He sees the Father do; for whatever He does, the Son also does in like manner" (John 5:19). He didn't come to originate a new model, but to mirror to this world the model already set by His Father. This is certainly true for us as well. There's a wonderful simplicity and exhilaration in going through each day knowing and reflecting Christ as the overriding priority for every situation.

He was dependent upon the Father's *will.* "I can of Myself do nothing. As I hear, I judge; and My judgment is righteous, because I do not seek My own will but the will of the Father who sent Me" (John 5:30). His will was always subservient to that of His Father, even at the times His humanity pushed Him in other directions. "Nevertheless not My will, but Yours, be done" (Luke 22:42). We, too, are called to the vibrant rest of taking Christ's yoke upon us and abandoning our wills to His perfect direction.

He was also dependent upon the Father's *power.* "The Father who dwells in Me does the works" (John 14:10). Christ forever puts to rest the thought of working for God. Even *He* didn't work this way. The accomplishments of His life were borrowed accomplishments—God-originated and God-produced. This must also be true for us if the touch of God is going to be felt through our lives. Our achievements are to be, like Paul's, "things which Christ has…accomplished through me, in word and deed" (Romans 15:18).

At every turn Christ looked to see where God was heading, to mirror only God's example, to fulfill only God's desire, and to do all of it only in God's power.

His design for us is the same: "Peace to you! As the Father has sent Me, I also send you" (John 20:21). Our lives are to be lived out in the same desperate, unceasing dependence on Christ that Christ has on God.

And therein lies our greatest problem.

WORKING FOR GOD OR WITH GOD?

Sin has cunningly introduced into the world the outrageous proposition that man can do life without God; that by our own wisdom and through our own strength we can make life work. Yet sin has also introduced a similar deception to the church—that *Christians can do ministry without God*, that by our own wisdom and through our own strength we can make ministry succeed. No one would own up to believing that, of course, but it's happening far more than we want to admit. A few examples:

- We rely more on planning meetings than seasons of prayer in developing vision and strategies for our church.
- Our response to financial shortfall is a stewardship campaign rather than an honest appraisal of where those of us in leadership may be quenching the Spirit.
- Our sermons become more concerned about cultural relevance than soundly and relevantly communicating the Word of God.
- Our services are seeker-driven rather than glory-driven. (I deeply appreciate the many good things about the seeker church model, but the most central calling of any body of believers is not to be seeker-sensitive, but to be God-flaunting—to extol and exalt His unrivaled excellencies. Also, the most loving thing we can do for any unbeliever is clearly expose them to the awesome and remarkable God before whom they must one day stand.)
- We're more concerned that the Sunday morning service end on time than that the Spirit be given freedom to continue working among God's people.
- We refuse, at the leadership level, to joyously decentralize ministry and entrust it to others.
- We find ourselves relying more on the training we received than on the Lord Himself.
- We read our Bibles without praying for understanding.

- When we pray without asking the Lord to direct and energize our prayers.

These are but a few telltale signs that we're working for God rather than with God.

When I use that phrase "with God," I don't mean a kind of 50-50 situation where God does half the work and we do the other half. Over the years I've heard the advice many times: "Pray as if it all depended on God; work as if it all depended on you." That's exactly *not* what it means to work with God. *All* of the work is His—every bit of it. From beginning to end it's all His energy, His wisdom, His flow, His love, and ultimately His success. But it's done through all of us. He uses our hands, our feet, our sweat, our tears.

It's really a 100-100 situation—all of God through all of us. As Paul said, "But by the grace of God I am what I am, and His grace toward me was not in vain; but I labored more abundantly than they all, yet not I, but the grace of God which was with me" (1 Corinthians 15:10). Note Paul's emphasis: "I labored more abundantly than they all"—100 percent Paul. "Yet not I, but the grace of God which was with me"—100 percent God.

I say it again: True ministry is all God's work from beginning to end, done through all of us. Or in the image of rivers within, it's God's flood through our floodgates.

What will it take, then, for our floodgate to be opened wide so that the indwelling life of Christ can spill forth to those on the outside? Let's look at three key hinges upon which the floodgate of our life turns— brokenness, dependence, and yieldedness.

BROKENNESS

The first hinge upon which the floodgate of supernatural influencing turns is brokenness—the true humility that comes from seeing all that I am in the light of all that God is.

Isaiah became a broken man only when he saw himself in the full blaze of God's blinding and shattering holiness. Only then did he cry out, "Woe is me, for I am undone! Because I am a man of unclean lips, and I dwell in the midst of a people of unclean lips; for my eyes have seen the King, the LORD of Hosts" (Isaiah 6:5).

"The true way to be humble," wrote Phillips Brooks, "is not to stoop until you're smaller than yourself, but to stand at your real height against some higher nature that will show you what the real smallness of your greatness is."[3] True humility is never developed by thinking ourselves down. It comes by bringing all our goodness, all our talents, all our accomplishments and standing tiptoe against the nature of God. In that comparison and contrast, our confidence in self and our pride in our abilities are ground to dust. In the rubble of that shattered hubris, God can now begin to work.

Brokenness is the soil from which all the genuine good in our lives springs forth. "God creates out of nothing," Martin Luther reminds us. "Therefore until a man is nothing, God can make nothing out of him."

To that I would add, "or do anything through him." John Ruskin calls humility "the first test of a truly great man," and observes that "really great men have a…feeling that the greatness is not in them but through them, that they could not do or be anything else than God made them." Only broken people realize that greatness isn't *in* them, but comes *through* them from God.

So God pays special attention to those who are broken: "But on this one will I look: on him who is poor and of a contrite [literally, 'shattered'] spirit, and who trembles at My word" (Isaiah 66:2). It's with the broken that He promises to take up special residence and give special refreshing. "For thus says the High and Lofty One who inhabits eternity, whose name is Holy: 'I dwell in the high and holy place, with him who has a contrite and humble spirit, to revive the spirit of the humble, and to revive the heart of the contrite ones'" (Isaiah 57:15).

God uses the broken in special ways as well: "When you were little in your own eyes, were you not head of the tribes of Israel?" (1 Samuel 15:17). Nothing is more fundamental to knowing God, enjoying God, experiencing God's power, and being used for God's purposes than this crucial though elusive commodity called brokenness.

Desperate Neediness

But what does brokenness look like? While it often involves sorrow and remorse over our sins, I don't think those are its primary attributes. I believe brokenness has far more to do with absence of confidence than anguish of heart. Larry Crabb writes, "Brokenness is the admission that the flesh is utterly insufficient for the job it has taken on."[4] It has to do with a spirit utterly drained of self-sufficiency, self-independence, self-glorification. It maintains a desperate sense of its ongoing neediness for anything genuinely good to come from us.

Brokenness is the condition expressed in the first beatitude: "Blessed are the poor in spirit, for theirs is the kingdom of heaven" (Matthew 5:3). It's what Paul was alluding to when he cried out, "For I know that in me (that is, in my flesh) nothing good dwells" (Romans 7:18).

Our flesh can so easily deceive us into trusting things other than the Lord Himself alone. C. S. Lewis noted that our problem isn't trusting God; it's in trusting God *only.* The more our movement toward others is energized by dependence upon a conglomerate (God plus other things), the less possibility there is for the sheer, naked power of the Holy Spirit to break through.

We all have areas in our lives that could be considered natural strengths. Perhaps you were blessed with a bright intellect. Great! Thank God for it—and then get over it. The greatest intellect, as great a gift as it can be, isn't one iota less dependent upon the Holy Spirit for illumination than anyone else. "There is no worse screen to block out the Spirit," John Calvin wrote, "than confidence in our own intelligence."[5]

Martin Luther noted this as well:

It is very certain that we cannot attain to the understanding of
Scripture, either by study or by the intellect. Your first duty is to
begin by prayer. Entreat the Lord to grant you, of His great mercy,
the true understanding of His Word. There is no other interpreter
of the Word of God than the Author of this Word, as He Himself
has said: "They shall all be taught of God." Hope for nothing from
your own labors, from your own understanding: trust solely in God,
and in the influence of His Spirit. Believe this on the word of a man
who has had experience.[6]

Luther isn't diminishing the role of diligent study in exploring God's
Word. But when we read our Bibles without pleading for the Spirit's illumi-
nation, we betray a lingering confidence in our flesh that we can understand
God's eternal truths through the medium of our finite, earthbound minds.

Self-discipline that merely grits our teeth and is rigid, unavailable, and
quietly smug is the counterfeit to the true self-control that is one of the
fruits of the Spirit (see Galatians 5:22-23).

Strong or winsome personality can subtly quench our reliance on the
Spirit to reflect Christ into the world. Christian leadership can all too
easily be motivated by the unchecked ambitions of the flesh rather than
the unavoidable call of God.

"A true and safe leader," A. W. Tozer says, "is likely to be one who has no
desire to lead, but is forced into a position of leadership by the inward pressure of the Holy Spirit and the press of external situation." He continues:

Such were Moses and David and the Old Testament prophets. I
think there was hardly a great leader from Paul to the present day
but was drafted by the Holy Spirit for the task, and commissioned

by the Lord of the Church to fill a position he had little heart for.
I believe it might be accepted as a fairly reliable rule of thumb that
a man who is ambitious to lead is disqualified as a leader. The true
leader will have no desire to lord it over God's heritage, but will be
humble, gentle, self-sacrificing and altogether as ready to follow as
to lead, when the Spirit makes it clear that a wiser and more gifted
man than himself has appeared.[7]

Christian training, important as it is, can become a subtle danger.
Christian schools, seminaries, discipleship groups can all be a great blessing, but they cannot substitute for Christ Himself. Yet how readily we fall
back on skill sets, training techniques, a body of doctrine, and principles
for effective ministry rather than relying on the Lord Himself. Certainly
He can use these tools and training for His purposes, and when we allow
Him to work through them, they've played their proper role. But when a
difficult or challenging situation arises and we begin to think, *Now what
was I trained to do? Which principle should I put in action here?* we revert to
what I like to call "flow-chart spirituality." In essence, it's looking to our
training with the same passion and dependence that we ought to be looking to our Lord.

Equally dangerous is a subtle reliance on our gifts rather than on the
Gift Giver. Charles Haddon Spurgeon, one of the most gifted preachers in
church history, said that whenever he went up to preach he repeated under
his breath, "I believe in the Holy Spirit, I believe in the Holy Spirit."
Without the energizing influence of the Holy Spirit, our gifts can never be
utilized for their intended purpose.

Embracing Your Inadequacy

So much of what we're looking at here is the unreserved embracing of our
inadequacy. Almost all of us will agree that we're inadequate. But too often

we're only giving mental assent to our inadequacy, then feverishly working to prove that we aren't that bad off. We are, at best, merely shaking hands with our inadequacy rather than passionately embracing it. Yet living life with this profound sense of not having what it takes is the starting point for experiencing the flow of God through our lives.

As Nancy Leigh DeMoss asks in *Brokenness: The Heart God Revives,* "Do you want the power of God to flow through you?… Revival is really nothing more than the release of God's Spirit through broken lives."[8]

I've found the greatest sense of the Spirit's presence and power during those times when I've been most deeply aware of my utter bankruptcy. The first funeral service I ever led was for a man in our church who had committed suicide. I had no idea what to say or what direction to go with the eulogy. I so clearly remember falling on my knees and crying out, "God, I so, so need You. I don't know what to say, how to address the issue of suicide, or how to even begin to comfort his wife and children." That was the starting point of the Lord carrying me through, giving me a message, and enabling me to flow into his family's life, at least in some measure.

In reality, my neediness on that occasion was no greater than it is at any other time; I was just more aware of it. Only when we passionately embrace our bankruptcy and neediness will the floodgate of our lives begin to open up to the flow of God.

DEPENDENCE

Dependence is the second hinge on the floodgate of our lives. This is the flip side of brokenness in working with God. If brokenness is the deep distrust we have in our own native abilities to do anything of eternal significance for God, then dependence is the wholesale reliance we have on God alone to do through us all that He asks of us. Brokenness is humbly recognizing the depths of our own personal bankruptcy; dependence is confidently drawing upon the fullness of our wealth in Christ. We must have both. Brokenness without dependence will lead only to spiritual morbidity. Dependence without brokenness will lead to spiritual elitism.

To abide in Christ must always involve brokenness: "As the branch cannot bear fruit of itself.... Without Me you can do nothing" (John 15:4-5). Yet it will always involve dependence as well: "He who abides in Me, and I in him, bears much fruit" (15:5).

The whole of our Christian experience is designed by God to be a testimony to the unrivaled power of divine intervention. Our spiritual success never hinges upon our stepping out to work for Him, but upon our stepping back to allow Him to supernaturally intervene in our place. As we saw before, this doesn't mean we aren't vitally involved in the whole affair, but it does mean that from beginning to end it is His work, His wisdom, His love, and His power that carry the day.

"There is an absolute and universal dependence of the redeemed on God," writes Jonathan Edwards. "The redeemed are in every thing directly, immediately, and entirely dependent on God: they are dependent on him for all, and they are dependent on him every way."[9]

How do we know whether we're deeply depending upon God?

I would say that this is always a growing part of our Christian lives. As we mature in Christ we discover more and more the subtle ways we make flesh our strength (see Jeremiah 17:5) and unwittingly quench the Spirit (see 1 Thessalonians 5:19). Sooner or later we discover there's no such thing as residual spirituality. Our Christian growth doesn't build up a surplus of spiritual vitality that resides with us whether we're relying on the Lord or not. Every moment, every temptation, every situation, every opportunity requires immediate and desperate dependence upon the Spirit of God for true good to come forth.

C. S. Lewis noted this in a letter to a friend:

As you say, the thing is to rely *only* on God. The time will come when you will regard all this misery as a small price to pay for

having been brought to that dependence. Meanwhile (don't I know)
the trouble is that relying on God has to begin all over again every
day as if nothing had yet been done.[10]

While dependence involves many things, one central feature towers
above all the rest—prayer. It seems to me that prayer is the single greatest
litmus test for the reality of our dependence.

I don't mean just a prayer time in the morning or evening (important
as that can be), but prayer as a way of life—continually calling out to
God, usually silently, as we go through the day, asking for His wisdom and
strengthening at every turn.

I'm convinced that the reason we don't pray more is never that we're
too busy; it's always that we're too confident. When God opens our eyes to
our abject neediness in everything that truly matters, prayer becomes radically more than a spiritual discipline or cultivated habit; it becomes the
soul's ongoing gasp for the air only God can provide.

Too often our daily spiritual lives are carried out in what I like to call
the "gas station" approach. We spend time with the Lord in the morning,
get our tanks filled, then go out to meet the day by drawing off the morning's strength. A few hours into our day, the strength and joy of the morning quiet time have usually faded, and we're back on our own.

The genuinely dependent saint runs more like the trolley. He or she is
connected to the higher Power Source throughout the entirety of the day,
drawing continuously at every turn.

The issue isn't so much the praying as the radical dependence on God
and deep distrust in self that the prayers reflect. It's the believer's gasp for
air throughout the course of the day. This may well have been in Paul's
mind when he wrote, "Pray without ceasing" (1 Thessalonians 5:17).

Yet prayer is also more than our gasp for air; it's our heaviest artillery
for attacking Satan's strongholds. "Ministry is simply reaping the spoils of
battle won in prayer," as my friend, Rev. Charlie Boyd, expressed it. In the

context of spiritual warfare, Paul commands us to be "praying always with all prayer and supplication in the Spirit" (Ephesians 6:18). No wonder he said the top priority of any body of believers is "first of all that supplications, prayers, intercessions, and giving of thanks be made for all men" (1 Timothy 2:1).

"God does nothing but in answer to prayer," John Wesley said.[11] A later Methodist preacher, Samuel Chadwick, said that the devil's one concern "is to keep saints from prayer. He fears nothing from prayerless studies, prayerless work, prayerless religion. He laughs at our toil, mocks at our wisdom, but trembles when we pray."[12]

If we want to be men and women of supernatural influence, one of the most foundational pursuits of our lives must be Spirit-dependent, Spirit-energized prayer that links us dependently with God.

YIELDEDNESS

Yieldedness is the final hinge upon which our floodgate swings open. This, too, is a central component of abiding. The branch is dependent upon the vine not only for all its vitality but also for all its direction. The branch is subservient to the vine, not the vine to the branch.

This attitude of submission is critical to being a supernatural influencer. Does the vine (Christ) have the kind of sway in our lives that allows Him to take us where He wants, how He wants, and when He wants?

In the book of Romans, Paul opens the door to Christ flowing through us in significant, God-honoring service by entreating, "I beseech you therefore, brethren, by the mercies of God, that you present your bodies a living sacrifice, holy, acceptable to God, which is your reasonable service" (Romans 12:1). Christ is looking for living, breathing bodies through which He can walk, talk, work, and most of all, love. When He finds believers willing to yield their bodies to Him in this way, all heaven breaks loose.

Here's one of the most essential elements of white-water spirituality and godly influencing. It's the glorious adventure of pulling up all the stakes, going for broke, and launching out into the white water of God's movement in human history at this point and time. Our strength and happiness, wrote Henry Ward Beecher, "consists in finding out the way in which God is going, and going in that way too."[13]

So what does it mean, then, to pull up stakes and present our body a living sacrifice?

Several years ago the Lord impressed me with four words that go a long way in answering this question for me. I was in Guatemala with a team of college students on a short-term mission trip. We spent half a day alone with the Lord toward the end of that time, reflecting on what we'd seen and asking the Lord how He would have us respond. At the time I was wrestling with the question of whether He wanted me and my family to go overseas as missionaries or to stay in the States ministering as we were.

As I was praying, the Lord spoke to me that the greatest issue He was concerned about was not location (where geographically to serve Him), but consecration (how yielded was I to what He wanted to do through me). Then He impressed me with four words for which He alone would provide the definition:

Whatever. Was I available to do whatever He called me to? Was I available to go overseas as a missionary? Or to be a college pastor the rest of my life? Or to go back into the working world to minister there?

Wherever. Was I willing to allow Him to determine my location? Or was I saying, "Lord, I'll serve You anywhere except…"? As long as I was geographically roping Him off from certain parts of the globe, I knew I could never be confident that I was where He wanted me to be.

Whenever. Was I waiting on His timetable? Was I open to being inconvenienced by His timing and His override on my plans?

However. Was I willing to be supported however He chose? Was I willing to raise support if He called us overseas? Was I willing to work part-time if that was His calling?

Someone has defined *Lord* as "the One who has the final say." That's what this issue of yieldedness is all about. If we can stay genuinely open to letting the Lord define the specifics of those words, we'll be a long way down the road toward being a living sacrifice.

This is an ongoing process for us all, and painful at times. Satan would have us view each of these words as sheer personal suicide or as a foolhardy risk, when life can be managed so much more safely and comfortably if we just hold on. Holding on, however, is the most foolhardy and ultimately the most tragic personal suicide. Because nothing can match the deep-seated satisfaction, the soul-stirring adventure, and the unreasonable joy of a life lived with the floodgates wide open.

Paul called this kind of life our "reasonable [literally, 'logical'] service." When we understand what is at stake in the full yielding of our bodies to Christ, it's indeed foolhardy to hang on, regardless of the risks. For when life is lived without risk, it's no longer life. It's merely existence. Life comes when we can launch out into each day guided by the words of the old Franciscan prayer:

> Lord, take me where you want me to go;
> Let me meet who you want me to meet,
> Tell me what you want me to say,
> And then keep me out of the way.

Divine Masterpieces

If souls do not shine before you it is because
you bring them no light to make them shine.
CANNON FARRAR

Years ago, an artist in Paris would go from park to park on the weekends to sketch portraits for anyone willing to pay his price. One Sunday when he couldn't find any interested customers, he happened to notice a drunk slumped on a park bench. The artist decided to draw a portrait of this disheveled individual, except that it would show what he envisioned the man would look like if his life were reformed. He drew the man as clean shaven, well groomed, and in a fine suit.

When he finished, he asked the man to come over and look at the drawing. The man staggered over, looked at it, then complimented the artist on his work. Looking around the park, he asked, "But where is this man?"

"The man is you," the artist answered.

The drunk was initially offended, believing the artist to be making fun of him. But the artist assured him this wasn't the case and pled with him to look more closely at the picture. Sure enough, as the man gazed upon the portrait he saw himself unmistakably there, though in a condition far different from his present one.

Tears began streaming down his face. No one had ever seen him in this light before, and hope stirred in his heart that perhaps he could actually become the man in the portrait.

He turned to the artist and said through his tears, "If that's the man you see, then that's the man I'll be." And according to tradition that's what happened. He reformed his way of living and before long became the very man whom the warm-hearted artist had drawn.

Perspective is an incredibly powerful thing. Because this artist made the effort to envision *what could be* in spite of *what was* in a slumping drunk, he was able to have dramatic influence on the man's life.

SEEING WHAT COULD BE

The ability to visualize what is not immediately apparent helps provide the inspiration for pursuing what might otherwise seem impossible. Walt Disney died before he ever saw the completion of his great undertaking, Disney World. At the park's grand opening, one Disney executive commented to another, "If only Uncle Walt could have been here to see this!" The other responded insightfully, "He did, that's why it's here." And he was right.

In this chapter we want to look at the power of perspective as we seek to be used by God in having divine impact in others' lives. We've seen that our goal in supernaturally influencing others is to work with God in helping them fulfill their whole potential in Christ. But how is this done?

To a great extent, we do it through (1) strengthening and nourishing their new nature, (2) exposing the perversity and insanity of living by their old nature, and (3) beckoning them to a more God-honoring and personally satisfying plane of living. This isn't meant to serve as a formula for spiritual impact; rather it gives three critical areas to keep in mind as we're asking God where and how He would flow through us into the lives of other saints.

Before we begin addressing the divine practice of strengthening, exposing, and beckoning, we must first start with the divine perspective through which God would have us view all believers.

How are we to look upon the believers God has placed in our lives? Do we see them more as sinners or as saints? Are we focused more on the baggage they bring or the new nature they possess? What things can we assume about them because they're new creations in Christ and have the Spirit of the living God dwelling within? Or to put it another way, what kind of material has God given us to work with?

This is no academic issue. We treat things we believe to be of great value and potential much differently than we treat those that seem to be of little worth or minimal potential. You would care for a five-carat diamond far differently than you would a mere cubic zirconia. A Rembrandt original would receive a certain kind of treatment in your house that other paintings would not.

What we learn from the Scriptures is that every believer is a Rembrandt in hiding. There are no cubic-zirconia saints—only five-carat-diamond ones.

This makes a radical difference in the way we view and relate to fellow brothers and sisters in Christ. Do we see them as they could be or as they are? God calls each of us to the great joy and privilege of being His sketch artists on earth, helping other believers recognize the God-infused beauty He has placed within them and beckoning them to the God-created potential for which they were made.

MONUMENTS TO GOD'S GRACE

The New Covenant requires that we gaze upon other believers through fundamentally optimistic lenses. "Therefore, from now on, we regard no one according to the flesh," Paul said (2 Corinthians 5:16). We no longer have the option of viewing other believers only, or even primarily, in light of their humanity or sinfulness. No Christian is fundamentally a slumped-over sinner, though it may appear that way from the outside. We aren't sinners in need of fixing so much as saints in need of releasing. Every saint has a drastic God dimension that can never be eradicated or even diminished. This God dimension is to be primary in our focus on one another.

Paul went on to give his first example of what it means not to view someone according to the flesh: "Even though we have known Christ according to the flesh, yet now we know Him thus no longer" (5:16). Do we think of Jesus Christ now as a carpenter from Nazareth or an itinerant teacher from Galilee? Obviously not. We think of Him as the resurrected, living Lord of the universe. He's an ongoing, unwavering exhibition of resurrection power. What's most fundamental to Him is unbridled, unrestrained deity.

That's what makes the "therefore" so significant in the next verse: "Therefore, if anyone is in Christ, he is a new creation; old things have passed away; behold, all things have become new" (5:17). Just as Jesus is the ongoing scene of resurrection power, so is every believer whether we behave like it or not. *Every Christian is a walking miracle!* Some of us live more like limping miracles, but the problem isn't on the end of what God has supplied, but on the end of what we've appropriated. Augustine once wrote in his journal after he'd committed a particular sin, "Thou fool, knowest not that thou carriest around God in thy body?" Oh, that we could take hold of that more consistently in viewing both ourselves and others.

Notice that Paul didn't say old things *are* passing away and all things *are* becoming new. No, something far more radical has occurred—a revolution within of monumental proportions. Fellow brothers and sisters in Christ are not just forgiven sinners! They're living, breathing monuments to the eternal and present grace of God. Within every believer lies something deeper than greed, lust, insecurity, arrogance, or addictions. What's deeper is their new, God-wrought purity, identity, disposition, and power. Nothing can alter or even diminish that supernatural reality.

Often, however, we become so focused on believers' shortcomings that we lose sight of the greater reality lurking beneath the surface—their new nature through the Holy Spirit. According to tradition, Michelangelo sculpted his masterpiece *David* from a piece of marble that other artists had discarded as useless. When asked where he got his inspiration for the sculpture, he replied, "I looked at the rock and saw an angel trapped inside." As he worked, it was always with the perspective of drawing out from the marble what he believed was already there, not creating something that didn't yet exist.

This is the perspective God would have us held hostage by as we view other believers. It isn't a naive, blindly optimistic view that fails to see the sin. It looks sinfulness fully in the face, willing to deal with it as the Spirit directs. But it always keeps its eyes on the angel trapped inside, the drastic God-dimension lurking beneath. "My little children," Paul wrote, "for whom I labor in birth again *until Christ is formed in you*" (Galatians 4:19).

As we participate with God in releasing the trapped angel, we do so in reliance upon certain divine realities He would have us capitalize upon. He has given us some great clay to work with, but we must know something of its composition to properly affect it.

Their Divine Purpose

Because of what God has done in the soul of every believer, we can make two central assumptions about any Christian. (And by the way, if your children are believers, this is just as true for them.) These assumptions are critical for influencing others from the relaxed strength and vibrant rest of New Covenant relating.

The first assumption we can make about every fellow believer concerns their divine purpose: *This person is designed to reflect God's beauty and do works He prepared for them before time began.* "For we are His workmanship, created in Christ Jesus for good works, which God prepared beforehand that we should walk in them" (Ephesians 2:10). This tells me there are no insignificant saints, no disposable believers, no unimportant children of God. John Ruskin wrote, "No man is without a divinely appointed task, and a divinely bestowed strength adequate for its fulfillment."

Every believer is of immense value and importance. Not just because Christ died for them, but also because He wants to hold them forth as living, breathing exhibitions of His unrivaled grace and power. "For we are His workmanship..." Literally, we're His *poiema,* His poem. We're His divine exhibition of spiritually creative and supernaturally inscribed penmanship. As the old preacher put it, "God don't make no junk." Every one of us is handcrafted by God to be a public display of Christ's beauty, a billboard for the kingdom of God. "And they glorified God in me" (Galatians 1:24) is to be true of us as much as it was of Paul.

Beyond this, every believer has a sum total of good works God has designed and designated to be done through his or her life: "created in Christ Jesus for good works, which God prepared beforehand that we should walk in them" (Ephesians 2:10). From eternity past, God has sovereignly laid out all the good deeds He wants distributed through our lives. We don't appear on the stage of life with an empty script, then try to figure out good things to do for God's production. Our script is already written; our part is already designated. Our calling now is to be sensitive and available to the movement of the Spirit in and through our lives. Or in the words of Christ, to "abide."

He has given to every believer one or more spiritual gifts (see 1 Peter 4:10) to utilize in the carrying out of His plan for us. Like our Lord, true success is found in being able to say, "I have glorified You on the earth. I have finished the work which You have given Me to do" (John 17:4).

Talk about significance in life! Designed to refract God's glory into this dark world and to have part in a work that will last for eternity! Whenever you and I look at another believer, I wonder if we have any real concept of the significance that person holds and the awesome potential he or she possesses for the kingdom of God. How easily we dismiss certain believers because of their failures, yet forget that God uses only failure-familiar saints like you and me.

No Baggage Too Heavy

This is one reason I would love to see the church drop any distinction between "counseling" and "discipleship." Too often, counseling is viewed as helping the people with really serious problems and trying to get them stabilized, while discipleship is equipping the more healthy believers for going out into battle for the kingdom. What a tragic and thoroughly un-biblical distinction! We're all walking wounded in need of help, and we're all called by God to positions on the battlefield, regardless of our wound-edness. Let's call it all one thing—"mentoring" perhaps, or "shepherd-ing"—since it's all part of the same great issue, becoming like Christ.

My experience over the years has been that many of those who went through "counseling" have become significant warriors for the kingdom because their brokenness drove them to desperately draw off the Lord's resources. Sometimes, others who have been "discipled" had significant, unaddressed issues in life that they either were unaware of or unwilling to look at, and these issues continue to hinder their true discipleship.

Let's beware of writing off any believer because he or she seems to have too much baggage; no baggage is too heavy for God to carry. And let's also keep in mind that the only "healthy" saints are broken saints, and we all have issues that warrant a lifetime of brokenness.

Many years ago when I was a pastor to college students, my wife began meeting with a young woman in our group who was painfully shy, desperately fearful, and had a difficult past. To my shame, I must confess that I mentally dismissed her as someone who would probably never have much influence for the kingdom of God.

Fortunately, my wife saw her in a far different light. She spent countless hours on the phone with her, walked with her as she worked through many difficult issues, and just loved her well. Beneath this young woman's fears and insecurity, my wife could see a rare courage and integrity before God. She began to blossom in ways I never would have dreamed possible.

When she graduated she was offered a job that was a frightening challenge for her. But because it afforded her great opportunities for sharing the gospel, she took it. Out of her brokenness, God has turned her into a radiant woman of God who is having significant ministry to this day. She's one of the most overt demonstrations of resurrection power I know. Meanwhile, some of her college peers who seemed at the time so on-fire for the Lord, with such promising potential for His work, are today nowhere to be seen, spiritually speaking.

I learned two of my greatest lessons in ministry by watching my wife with this young college girl. First, *none of us is omniscient enough to know where any believer may end up.* And second, *nothing in a person's life is too heavy for the Spirit of God to move.* The issue is never the amount of fleshly baggage in people's life, but whether they'll avail themselves of the manifold resources of the Spirit, which are always deeper and ultimately more powerful than the baggage.

Let's remember also that every believer has a giftedness that's different from our own. We must be careful not to place our agenda upon them, mistakenly attempting to move them toward fulfilling what *we think* is the good and acceptable and perfect will of God for their life. A New Covenant approach toward influencing others is concerned with helping them hear the voice of God *for themselves* and to find the unique calling God has designed *for them.* Our calling isn't to mold them into saints who fit within our framework for spirituality. It's to release them to the far greater and infinitely more important calling of fitting into God's framework for their lives here on earth, regardless of how different that may look from ours.

Another way to express it is that we're to view other believers *transcendently*. This word comes from the Latin *transcendere*, which means "to go beyond." Every believer's life is designed to count for something beyond this time and this place. There's always something greater at stake in our lives than our present pleasures or pains. That something is the glory of God.

More than anything else, the fiery concern for His reputation can help us move meaningfully toward those believers we don't naturally enjoy or who intimidate us or whom we have written off because of their struggles.

When God called Ananias to go to the newly converted Saul of Tarsus, he was less than pleased with the assignment, to say the least. He articulated strong reasons for not going. Yet God wouldn't budge. Why did God insist that Ananias go? Was it His love for Saul? Or Saul's neediness? No. God instructed Ananias, "Go, for he is a chosen vessel of Mine *to bear My name* before Gentiles, kings, and the children of Israel" (Acts 9:15). Ananias was to go not because of what it would do for him or even for Saul, but because of what it would do for God's name.

Be a Burning Bush

This preeminent concern for God's name will be a critical paradigm shift for many of us, especially when we're ruthlessly honest about our motivations for ministry. Why do we want to be used of God to help and influence others? Is it because we want to see their lives bettered? Is it because we want to taste the deep joy and satisfaction of God working through us? Is it because we want to be well rewarded at the judgment seat of Christ? All these are legitimate secondary motivations. But secondary they are, and secondary they must always remain. What matters supremely in our involvement with others is not what it does for us or even for them, but what it does for seeing God's fame rightly recognized and adored on earth.

Few things are so freeing, so invigorating, so emboldening, and ultimately so love-producing as being caught up in a God-bestowed jealousy for how this person before me can serve as a flesh-and-blood attention-getter for the unrivaled supremacy of our God. This divine jealousy isn't something for us to work up, but rather to fall back on. It's an indwelling fire in every Christian, for the central passion of the Spirit within us is to spotlight Christ (see John 16:14). As we allow ourselves to indulge the deepest desire of our new heart, we'll find that nothing matters more or satisfies more deeply than the breathtaking wonder and stunning spectacularness of the true and living God. And nothing can elevate and ennoble our lives more than being used on this earth to advance that wonder and spectacularness among men.

This truth of the centrality of God's glory continues to revolutionize my view of ministry. I try to think of every believer I come in contact with as a potential "burning bush." This image comes from the account of Moses on the backside of the desert where he encountered such an unusual sight: "The Angel of the LORD appeared to him in a flame of fire from the midst of a bush. So he looked, and behold, the bush was burning with fire, but the bush was not consumed" (Exodus 3:2).

Notice the response Moses had to this supernatural phenomenon: "I must turn aside now and see this marvelous sight, why the bush is not burned up" (3:3, NASB). Something about this bush stopped Moses in his tracks, and that something was God inside it.

All of us are called to be burning bushes in our generation, men and women whose lives cause others to stop in their tracks and wonder about what makes us tick. What caught Moses' attention wasn't the bush, but the fiery presence within it. That's also our calling and privilege. What matters most about our lives is not that people are drawn to admire what fine, upstanding bushes we are. It's that they're struck by the fiery presence within our bush, so much so that their light view of God is temporarily disrupted. This is what Christ was referring to when He said, "Let your light so shine before men, that they may see your good works and glorify your Father in heaven" (Matthew 5:16). Notice that He didn't say "Let your light shine," but "Let your light *so* shine." Live in such a way that people's attention quickly bounces off us and onto the God who is the only possible explanation behind our behavior.

In his classic work *The Saving Life of Christ*, Major Ian Thomas has a chapter entitled "Any Old Bush Will Do!" Any man, any woman, any child can be a burning bush for God in their generation, regardless of their past or present. You and I can be part of no greater cause than working with God to see His divine fire burning brightly in the lives of others, regardless of who they are or what position they hold.

Learning to see other saints primarily in light of their potential for exuding God's glory (and only secondarily in light of their own needs and faults) has been a critical change for me. It rebukes me when I'm tempted to think of any Christian as ordinary. "God has shown me that I should not call any man common" (Acts 10:28). The presence of God within every believer means that any life holds extraordinary possibilities. It reminds me that there's no such thing as a routine day of ministry. There's no telling when or how God's glory may be affected by the events and interactions of the day. Beyond this, it helps me in moving toward other believers whom I'm not naturally drawn to; it reminds me of the monumental significance of what's genuinely at stake.

THEIR SOURCE OF INTERNAL SATISFACTION

The second assumption we can make about other believers has to do with their internal satisfaction: *This person will never be deeply or fully satisfied until his or her life is fully caught up in the flow of God.*

No matter how attractive and satisfying things may look on the outside, some measure of internal restlessness and dissatisfaction will inevitably persist in the life of a believer who is out of alignment with God's presence and purposes. Jesus said that there's only one pathway to fullness of joy. "These things I have spoken to you, that my joy may remain in you, and that your joy may be full" (John 15:11). "These things" He's referring to is John 15:1-10 and all that it means to abide in Christ.

God often uses our dissatisfaction and restlessness in life to get our attention. "How long will you falter [literally, 'limp'] between two opinions? If the LORD is God, follow Him; but if Baal, follow him" (1 Kings 18:21). In essence, God is saying, "How long will you live a crippled life? You can't move full out in either direction, so choose one or the other." Through Isaiah He asks, "Why do you spend money for what is not bread, and your wages for what does not satisfy? Listen carefully to Me, and eat what is good, and let your soul delight itself in abundance" (Isaiah 55:2). Or as God spoke through Haggai, "Consider your ways! You have sown much, and bring in little" (Haggai 1:5-6). Paul asked, "What has happened to all your joy?" (Galatians 4:15, NIV).

In all these cases God is using the discontent and dissatisfaction that have arisen from His people's wayward or misguided lives to woo them back to Himself. Their inescapable emptiness and undeniable sense of something missing are His trump card to prove that they're presently in the wrong game.

People's discontentment in life is one of the greatest tools we have in ministry. God capitalizes upon it, and He calls us to do the same.

My wife and I once visited Alcatraz and had a fascinating time touring the prison facilities. At one point our guide asked us the question, "What night do you think was the most difficult for the prisoners here?" My thought was Christmas or perhaps their birthday. His answer was New Year's Eve—that was when they could hear the sounds of partying coming from San Francisco across the bay waters like no other night of the year. It reminded them of the freedom they'd forfeited and of the life that was passing them by.

One of our roles in supernaturally influencing others is to be that voice that comes across the waters, whispering to fellow believers, "Are you genuinely satisfied with your life? Are you enjoying the Lord? Do you feel like your days are counting for something truly significant?" We can count on the fact that God will never allow them the depth and breadth of satisfaction they long for until it's coming from full abandonment to His flow in their lives.

It seems to me there are three primary ways to help expose and highlight this lack of deep satisfaction that stems from resisting God's flow in one's life.

The Backward Look

First, there's the backward look. This is what our Lord does in rebuking the church of Ephesus for straying from their first love (see Revelation 2:1-7). One of the crucial things He calls them to do is "Remember therefore *from where* you have fallen" (2:5). What He's telling them to do is mentally go back to those first days of being saved, the days of their "first love." He wants them to linger upon the memories of how sweet the Lord tasted then, of the great joy they used to experience, of the vibrant rest that they were reveling in. The fond memories of life lived in vital intimacy with their Lord would serve to lure them back into the unfailing arms of Christ.

Paul did a similar thing in writing to the Galatians. The believers he was writing to had left the vibrant rest and joyous intimacy of living through a Person (see Galatians 1:6; 2:20) and had reverted to the old way of living under a code (4:9-11). They believed this new brand of spirituality was really an upgrade from what they'd received from Paul. So he asked them a penetrating question, "What has happened to all your joy?" (4:15, NIV). How can this new brand of Christianity really be an improvement when it has robbed your joy, overturned your peace (1:7), and drained your love (4:13-15)? Remembering what things were like at the beginning should drive you to deep discontent with how things are now.

I recently was chatting with a college student who had been drifting in his walk with the Lord. I asked him what he would call the time of greatest joy and contentment in his life. His response was that nothing compares with the day that he trusted Christ (as a boy with his parents) and the days immediately following. I then encouraged him to think hard about that time and juxtapose it with what things are like for him now. Why not go back to what brought you the best you've ever tasted?

Tragically, many Christians assume and are even taught that their first days in the faith are like their spiritual honeymoon. They're told that these initial feelings will fade and that what matters most from now on is ongoing commitment and faithfulness. We lay out for them a life of grim self-denial and label it with a most interesting word: *maturity.*

Neither our Lord nor Paul saw maturity this way. The joy and adventure of those first days as a believer are never meant to end, but to grow deeper and more sanctified. Suffering and heartache will inevitably be a major part of that deepening and sanctifying process, but they can't take away the vital joy that depends only upon intimate communion with our Lord. The first days and the first love can serve as a God-ordained anchor for drawing saints back to the only life they know has ever touched the deepest parts of their being and satisfied them as nothing else. "Then she will say, 'I will go and return to my first husband, for then it was better for me than now'" (Hosea 2:7).

The Present Look

The second means of revealing our dissatisfaction is the honest evaluation of the present to determine if the raging thirst in our soul is coming anywhere close to being quenched and if the gnawing hunger of our heart is being satisfied by the fare it is dining upon. This "present look" was what drew the prodigal son back home to his father: "How many of my father's hired servants have bread enough and to spare, and I perish with hunger! I will arise and go to my father" (Luke 15:17-18). The physical imagery of food in this parable is clearly meant to symbolize the spiritual realities of living life apart from Christ. It wasn't until the younger son recognized his desperate hunger that this dissatisfaction with the present drove him back into the arms of his father.

You'll find God focusing on the present discontent of His people again and again to draw them back to Himself. "Surely joy has withered away from the sons of men" (Joel 1:12); and only a deep return to Him can restore what they once enjoyed (see Joel 2:12-27).

The problem with idolatry is that the things and people of this world are "broken cisterns that can hold no water" (Jeremiah 2:13). The pleasures, possessions, or accomplishments this world provides to quench our thirst can never last long enough or settle deeply enough to be worth the effort. Only the Lord's cold, sparkling waters never run out. And until people recognize that their sin is not only a violation against God but also a foolish blunder against their own best interests, they usually will not change.

One of the ways God wants to use us in impacting others is to be His voice of reason to them, reminding them that their deepest longings are God-sized and God-implanted, and that the reason they aren't experiencing the depth of satisfaction they long for is the inevitable mismatch when we seek earth-sized pursuits to satisfy God-sized longings. "What does not satisfy when we find it," C. S. Lewis observed, "was not the thing we were desiring."[1] A crucial part of New Covenant ministry is not merely pointing out things that are wrong, but equally reminding why they can never satisfy.

The Forward Look

The third way of exposing our unmet desires is the forward look—pointing out what could be and how far it outstrips what presently is.

Again, we see this often in God's dealing with His people. He tells the idolatrous Israelites of Hosea's day that if they'll genuinely return to Him, He "will heal their backsliding" and "love them freely" and "be like dew to Israel"; they will "grow like the lily" and "be revived like grain" (Hosea 14:4-7).

Through the prophet Isaiah, God promises that if His people will open wide their floodgates in obediently offering help to the oppressed and needy, then "the LORD will…satisfy your soul in drought, and strengthen your bones; you shall be like a watered garden, and like a spring of water, whose waters do not fail" (Isaiah 58:11). The allurement of feasting on the best at God's table is a powerful incentive to give up the scraps that we too easily settle for.

I've found it helpful to highlight the testimonies of godly saints and their tasting of the Lord's fullness. Their fragrant and joyous accounting of the Lord's provision for their souls can be of tremendous help in letting go of the trinkets of this earth that are blocking our enjoyment of God's best.

During his last visit back to England, David Livingstone spoke to the students at Cambridge University. In his address he spoke these words concerning the sacrifices he'd made during his years in Africa:

> For my own part, I have never ceased to rejoice that God has appointed me to such an office. People talk about the sacrifice I have made in spending so much of my life in Africa. Can that be called a sacrifice which is simply paid back as a small part of a great debt owing to our God, which we can never repay? Is that a sacrifice which brings its own blest reward in healthful activity, the consciousness of doing good, peace of mind, and a bright hope of a glorious destiny hereafter? Away with the word in such a view, and with such a thought! It is emphatically no sacrifice. Say rather it is a privilege. Anxiety, sickness, suffering, or danger, now and then, with a foregoing of common conveniences and charities of this life, may make us pause, and cause the spirit to waver, and the soul to sink; but let this only be for a moment. All these are nothing when

compared with the glory which shall be revealed in and for us. I never made a sacrifice.[2]

Though Livingstone had been mauled by a lion, suffered innumerable sicknesses and wounds, and worked in almost constant jeopardy of his life, none of these things were what he remembered primarily about his years in Africa. He had tasted the vibrant rest and high adventure of white-water Christianity, a life lived with the floodgates wide open—and that overshadows everything.

SEEING WHAT'S MISSING

God created us with a God-shaped hole in our hearts, then rigged life in such a way that this hole can be filled only by the Person and purposes of Christ. We can bank on the fact that our Lord will not allow the deepest parts of our soul to experience vibrant rest while we're turning elsewhere to fill the hole.

Therefore, one of our key roles in supernaturally influencing others is to help them recognize that nameless, often vague but unmistakable sense of something missing in their lives. Then we must help them see that the only remedy for what's missing is to take the glorious risk of abandoning themselves to the currents of white-water spirituality.

So how do we view other believers, especially those who are struggling in their walk? As sinners who need to genuinely want what God offers and to begin doing the necessary spiritual things to get it? Or as saints whom God has already caused to want what He offers, but are sometimes thwarting His inward movement?

The second view was Paul's perspective. He told the Corinthian believers, "Clearly you are an epistle of Christ, ministered by us, written not with ink but by the Spirit of the living God, not on tablets of stone but on tablets of flesh, that is, of the heart" (2 Corinthians 3:3). He was fully confident that these saints had within them the desire to do God's will—that this desire had been written on their hearts by God's Spirit. But how did Paul know this?

The next verse gives the answer: "And we have such trust through Christ toward God" (3:4). The reason he was certain they wanted to do God's will was not their maturity, their discipline, or their commitment, but his "trust" that God, through Christ, had written His law unalterably on their hearts—one of the great provisions of the New Covenant.

God has given us more to work with in other believers' lives than most of us are aware of. Yes, our flesh is fallen; yes, it's depraved; yes, it does awful things. But there's much more than this in every believer's life. Through the indwelling Spirit, a dramatic and inerasable God-factor is waiting to be capitalized upon.

Let's begin exploring what this looks like.

The Heart Language of Influence

Give me the right word with the right accent
and I will move the world.

Joseph Conrad

Harry Winston was the world's greatest international jewel merchant of his day. Known as the King of Diamonds, he began his business in 1932 and became the world's leading seller of diamonds.

He once was watching one of his salesmen show a beautiful diamond to a rich Dutch merchant. The merchant listened carefully to the salesman's expert description of the diamond, then politely declined to buy it.

As the merchant was leaving, Winston stepped forward and asked if he might show him that diamond one more time. The merchant agreed. Harry took the stone in his hand and began talking about the stone as an object of deep beauty. Abruptly, the merchant changed his mind and purchased the diamond.

Later, as he was about to walk away with his purchase, the merchant turned to Winston and asked, "Why did I buy it willingly from you, though I had no difficulty saying no to your salesman?"

"That salesman is one of the best men in the business," Winston acknowledged. "He knows diamonds—but I love them."[1]

Ah, what a difference that makes. The speech of the heart is often louder and more convincing than actual words coming out of the mouth. This is especially true in the arena of spiritual influence. It's one thing to know people; it's a very different thing to love them. And the Spirit of God is working in each of our lives to turn us into spiritual Harry Winstons—true lovers of our Father's jewels, namely, His children. To have lasting influence upon His children, the language of the heart speaks the loudest.

THE RIGHT SPIRITUAL AMBIANCE

We saw earlier that every believer is a diamond in the rough, with an unalterable, God-bestowed beauty indwelling them. More specifically we saw two important things we can bank on in any true believer's life because of the work of the New Covenant in their heart: their divine purpose and their source of internal satisfaction. Now we want to begin looking at how to capitalize on these truths to further God's purposes in their lives.

Let's look first at the heart language through which all such things must be communicated. We often hear about the importance of both verbal and nonverbal communication in the overall process of getting our message across. In supernaturally influencing others, there's also something that perhaps is best described as "soul" or "heart communication." It's a spiritual ambiance that the Spirit of God wants to produce through us, an unspoken message that allows our actions and words to have maximum effect. This ambiance, however, is anything but a technique or skill. It requires the Spirit of God and is far more a heart issue than anything else.

Consider something that happened to a boy named John, who grew up in a Christian home and attended a Christian high school. He wasn't a rebellious kid, but he was somewhat irresponsible, and he did like to push the edge. He was in trouble fairly frequently and often visited the principal's office. Many labeled him a troublemaker, but that really wasn't his heart, deep down.

The school he attended required boys to always wear a belt in class. More than once John had forgotten his and suffered the consequences.

The school got a new principal, and he was warned about John. Sure enough, it looked like people were right: John came to school without his belt on the first day of classes under the new principal. Before the morning bell rang, he called John into his office.

John went in, and when the door closed, the principal said, "I noticed you aren't wearing a belt."

"No sir."

"If you go to class without one, you'll get in trouble, won't you?"

"Yes sir," John replied.

Then taking off his own belt, the principal handed it over to John.

"Here, why don't you wear this one today? Just give it back to me at the end of the day."

You probably won't be surprised to learn that this was the beginning of a wonderful relationship between that principal and John, a relationship that deeply impacted John and helped him turn back to the Lord. What power the language of the heart can have!

Whenever we interact with another person in any kind of significant way, it seems to me that there are four questions we're asking ourselves (usually unconsciously) about that person. Depending upon what we believe to be the answer to each of those questions, we're more open or more closed to their input in our lives. To the degree that these questions are answered no, our internal walls go up. To the degree they're answered yes, the walls tend to come down.

These questions aren't answered for us primarily by what a person says, but by an intuitive sense of who he or she is. Admittedly, this is a subjective kind of analysis, but we all live by it. To have a life-changing influence on others, this supernatural, spiritual ambiance is crucial. We need the right words but also the "right accent," as Joseph Conrad put it. And the right accent is a supernaturally derived heart language that's manifested in the following questions.

THE QUESTION OF GENUINE CONCERN

First, *does this person genuinely care about me as a person?* Or am I just a discipleship project or a means to further his own ends?

Whenever we sense that someone has an agenda to either fix us or use us, our walls inevitably go up. But when we sense that their desire is to better understand us and help however they can, the walls come tumbling down.

That's why the lifeblood of New Covenant influencing is a Spirit-generated, Christ-saturated love. Without the divine fragrance of this love scenting our words and actions, our opportunity for influence is dramatically lessened (see 1 Corinthians 13:1-3), and it's unlikely the people we're seeking to influence will let down their drawbridge so we may pass over into their lives. This is why we're to be "speaking the truth *in love*" (Ephesians 4:15).

A Christian man once went on a men's retreat with his church. That night when he went to bed he found the following note under his pillow, left by someone from a preceding group.

> Observations of a skeptic. I don't want to be told that God loves
> me or that Jesus loves me. I want to feel that the people who call
> themselves "Christian" love me. Then perhaps I can realize the love
> of God and the love of Christ. I don't want to be told about the

love of God and then find eyes averted when I look straight at a Christian.

I want to see God's love in eyes that are unafraid to look into mine, eyes that shine from a soul that is sincere. I want to experience God's love through a smile that says, "I love you, I accept you right where you are. I want genuinely to be your friend, now and when we leave this retreat place." Then maybe I can begin to believe in that love from God through this strange Christ that Christians talk so much about. And if I believe, then perhaps I too can live in love and give it to others. And, you know, I think I did find some of God's love here this weekend. Be ready on your retreat to receive it, and be ready to give it.

Peace,

Bob

No wonder God places such high emphasis upon love as our native language. This love, however, is always the fruit or by-product of the Spirit; we can't even remotely hope to accomplish something so Godlike without God Himself doing it through us.

Paul commended the Colossian believers for their "love for all the saints" (Colossians 1:4) while also giving their secret behind this love— "your love in the Spirit" (1:8).

"Love is a fruit," Max Lucado reminds us…

A fruit of whom? Of your hard work? Of your deep faith? Of your vigorous resolve? No, love is a fruit of the Spirit…. His job is to bear fruit. Our job is to stay put. The more tightly we are attached to Jesus, the more purely his love can pass through us.[2]

This Christ-engendered love will carry at least three central messages to those near us.

Love Never Fails

First, *I'm relentlessly and unconditionally for you. You can never quench my love for you.* Another way to say it: "My love toward you isn't predicated upon your faithfulness and service for God. You don't need to change in order to maintain my love."

It's like the love of our Lord who loved His disciples "to the end" (John 13:1). Or the love which "bears all things, believes all things, hopes all things, endures all things," and which refuses to give up—"never fails" (1 Corinthians 13:7-8).

As has often been observed, people don't care how much we know until they know how much we care. Think of the people who have most deeply influenced your life. Wasn't this genuine concern for you as a person one of the key ingredients that so powerfully touched you?

As I was growing up, one of the most influential men in my life was my tennis coach, who became a surrogate father to me (my own father died when I was five). He began coaching me when I was ten, and he remains a close friend to this day. What I remember so clearly from the first day I met him, and what impacted me so deeply, was the genuine concern and love he had for me as a person. He worked his players hard and sometimes yelled at us, and he often lectured me on various aspects of life and tennis. At times he said some hard things. But what I remember most was his broad smile, his continual encouragement, and the countless hours I spent with him and his wife outside of tennis. By my junior year in high school, I ate dinner more often at their house than my own. He taught me so many things, and he helped guide me in so many ways. And what kept me coming back for more was his genuine concern for me that I never doubted. Indeed "love never fails" (1 Corinthians 13:8).

This doesn't mean that this unconditional, relentless love might not be tough at times. It might even mean, if absolutely necessary, breaking fellowship with the loved one (1 Corinthians 5:11). But breaking fellowship is always to be done out of love, never because of a lack of it.

Whatever the situation, the key issue remains the same. Our ministry is to be bathed in a supernatural, relentless love for the ones God has given us the privilege and opportunity to influence.

Dinah Craik, nineteenth-century novelist, expressed it like this:

> Oh, the comfort, the inexpressible comfort, of feeling safe with a person, having neither to weigh thoughts nor measure words, but to pour them all out just as they are, chaff and grain together, knowing that a faithful hand will take and sift them, keep what is worth keeping, and then, with the breath of kindness blow the rest away.[3]

Love Sees What Can Be

This is another message that comes from Christ-engendered love: *I see your potential for the kingdom of God and it excites me. I'll do all I can to help see this potential realized.* The kind of love produced by the Holy Spirit is not only supernaturally unconditional but also divinely purposeful. We see love's ultimate target in these passages: "You did not choose Me, but I chose you and appointed you that you should go and bear fruit, and that your fruit should remain" (John 15:16). "My little children, for whom I labor in birth until Christ is formed in you" (Galatians 4:19).

True love provides both a home and a business. It provides a home in the sense that the loved one enjoys the warmth, strength, and respite of unconditional love. It provides a business in the sense that the loved one is loved with purpose-driven affection, encouraged toward fulfilling what he or she was made for.

It's critical that both be in place. Unconditional love that lacks purpose is soft and easily compromised. Purposeful love that's fettered with conditions is hard and easily fractured. Like our Lord, unconditional affection entwined with loving purposefulness is what this thing called "agape" is all about.

Love Fights Alongside

And here's another message: *I'll do all that I can to help inflame your new nature. I'll also stand against your flesh when necessary.* The writer of Hebrews exhorts us to "think hard about how to inflame one another to love and good works" (Hebrews 10:24, author's translation). One of the great purposes of our involvement with other saints is to help ignite one another's yearning for and commitment to supernatural living. It's also to stand against the flesh of beloved ones when they're drifting away. "Beware, brethren, lest there be in any of you an evil heart of unbelief in departing from the living God; but exhort one another daily, while it is called 'Today,' lest any of you be hardened through the deceitfulness of sin" (Hebrews 3:12-13).

Again, both are critical. We must seek both to inflame others' new nature as well as to stand against their old one. True love requires that we be wise physicians, knowing when and how to nourish the healthy tissue, and when and how to do battle against the cancer.

THE QUESTION OF RELIABILITY

The second heart-language question is this: *Can I trust that what this person is saying is really true?* This is why we're always to be "speaking *the truth* in love" (Ephesians 4:15).

This issue of truth has two primary components. One has to do with *content,* or the reliability of the information we're communicating. The other has to do with *character,* or the reliability of the integrity in what we're communicating.

The issue of information reliability is simply asking these questions: Is the information being communicated true? What's the source of the information? How reliable is that source?

Clearly this is an important reason for our lives to be bathed in

Scripture. To be a man or woman of God who is "complete, thoroughly equipped for every good work" requires a growing, personal grasp on the Word of God (see 2 Timothy 3:14-17). In admiration of John Bunyan, author of *Pilgrim's Progress,* Charles Spurgeon said, "Prick him anywhere, and you will find that his blood is Bibline." May the same be said of us. This doesn't mean that we're incessantly quoting Scripture, but that our outlook on life at every turn is inescapably colored by God's truth.

This doesn't require going to seminary or Bible college or going into "the ministry." Many of the men and women I've most respected and been most impacted by over the years did neither of these. But they knew the Word well from their own warm, personal walk with God.

Only the Word of God provides absolute truth (see John 10:35). Only the Word of God is promised not to return void (see Isaiah 55:11). It's only the Word of God that breaks rock in pieces (see Jeremiah 23:29), and only the Word of God is living and powerful and sharper than any two-edged sword (see Hebrews 4:12).

With the title "The Bible," John Greenleaf Whittier wrote these lines:

> We search the world for truth; we cull the good,
> The pure, the beautiful
> From all old flower fields of the soul;
> And, weary seekers of the best,
> We come back laden from our quest,
> And find that all the sages said
> Is in the Book our mothers read.[4]

Looking back on the momentous Reformation events of his lifetime in which he played such a crucial role, Martin Luther wrote this:

I simply taught, preached, wrote God's Word: otherwise I did noth-ing. And when, while I slept, or drank Wittenberg beer with my

Philip and my Amsdorf, the Word so greatly weakened the papacy that never a Prince or Emperor inflicted such damage upon it. I did nothing. The Word did it all.[5]

We can't be men and women of supernatural influence if we aren't humbly, winsomely, and wisely putting the Word of God out into circulation through our lives. "The law of truth was in his mouth, and injustice was not found on his lips. He walked with Me in peace and equity, and turned many away from iniquity" (Malachi 2:6). William Gladstone, prime minister of England said, "There is only one great issue and that is to get the truths of the Bible into the hearts of men." Regardless of our gifts, education, or station in life, we can all be about this eternally significant calling.

Meanwhile, the character issue—reliability of integrity—means asking this question: Has the information being communicated been twisted or altered in any way for personal gain?

Look at Paul's example in ministry:

For our exhortation did not come from error or uncleanness, nor was it in deceit. But as we have been approved by God to be entrusted with the gospel, even so we speak, not as pleasing men, but God who tests our hearts. For neither at any time did we use flattering words, as you know, nor a cloak for covetousness—God is witness. Nor did we seek glory from men. (1 Thessalonians 2:3-6)

If there are questions as to the underlying personal motives for what's being said, it will dramatically take away our ability to influence. People may not like what we have to say, but if they know it springs from an honest heart set on pleasing God above all else, they'll usually at least respect it.

This balance of love and truth is critical for having supernatural influence. Christ was full of grace *and* truth (see John 1:14). Truth without love, writes Joshua Swartz,

> is often intolerant and even persecuting, as charity without truth is
> weak in concession and untrustworthy in judgment. But charity,
> loyal to truth and rejoicing in it, has the wisdom of the serpent and
> the harmlessness of the dove.[6]

THE QUESTION OF COMMONALITY

Consider the third heart-language question: *Is this person speaking down to me as one already having arrived, or is he speaking alongside me as a fellow traveler?* It's difficult to hear others when they're speaking down to us from the mountaintop of mastery. This is where humility and brokenness become so important.

Concerning this very thing, Paul wrote, "Brethren, if a man is overtaken in any trespass, you who are spiritual restore such a one in a spirit of gentleness, *considering yourself lest you also be tempted*" (Galatians 6:1). My favorite definition of witnessing is "one beggar telling another beggar where to find bread." It's true in describing the whole of our Christian lives; we're always one struggler telling a fellow struggler where we found help.

In mentoring a friend, C. S. Lewis wrote, "Think of me as a fellow patient in the same hospital who, having been admitted a little earlier, could give some advice."[7] It makes such a difference when we approach people as fellow runners on the track rather than calling out instructions to them from the stands. This doesn't mean we can't speak with strong conviction at times, but the conviction needs to be drained of arrogance and of the pretense of having all our ducks in a row.

"The only way to help people," Alexander Maclaren writes,

is to get to their level. If you want to bless people, you must identify with them. It's no use standing on a pedestal above them, and patronizingly talking down to them. You cannot scold, or bully, or lecture men and women into the acceptance of religious truth if you take a position of superiority.[8]

This is one of my greatest concerns for those of us who are pastors, priests, and preachers. The physical setting in most churches requires that during the services the pastor talk down to the people in the congregation. We can so easily leave the impression that we're already doing all the things we're telling them to do. We all know how ridiculous that is. It's imperative that those communicating the Word of God do so as fellow strugglers in the Christian life. Open and discerning sharing of our own struggles in life and battles with the flesh can go a long way in this direction.

THE QUESTION OF REALITY

A final heart-language question is this: *Are the things this person is talking about a growing reality in his own life?* This doesn't mean perfection, but it does mean sincerity and progress. "Meditate on these things; give yourself entirely to them, that your progress may be evident to all" (1 Timothy 4:15). Paul wasn't commanding Timothy to be at a place of having fully arrived before doing ministry, just to be visibly hastening in that direction. James Russell Lowell wrote, "No man can produce great things who is not thoroughly sincere in dealing with himself."

The real issue here is *authenticity*, a commodity that's impossible to fake. People intuitively know whether it's there or not. When Billy Graham met Winston Churchill for the first time, it was for a brief moment in Churchill's office, with some of his cabinet members also present. After

Graham left the room, Churchill said to the others, "Now there goes a sincere man." The real thing can't be hidden, and its presence is crucial if others are to seriously consider our words.

These four questions serve, in many ways, as the drawbridge that allows us into other people's lives. Why is that? Because the answers to these questions signal the presence or absence of four key things we need to have toward one another if they're going to have access into our lives: respect, trust, safety, and an unmistakable sense of being cared about. These are crucial for being men and women of lasting influence.

Let me hasten to say that no one does any of these things perfectly. It's a growing process for all of us, myself very much included. The good news is that God always uses us *in spite* of ourselves, never *because.* This is no excuse for not seeking to grow in these areas, but simply a reminder that God still uses us even when our lives aren't all that they should be.

It could be easy to read this chapter and become buried with guilt because we don't fully measure up to these four things. Of course we don't. The answer isn't to let Satan paralyze us with shame, but to turn to God in new and more desperate ways, beseeching Him to work these things into our lives as only He can.

Joseph Conrad was right. We need the right word, but we also need the right accent. This accent is something only God can give through the working of the Holy Spirit in our hearts. But it's an accent that must be heard if our words and actions are to deeply penetrate. Let's now begin looking at those words and actions.

Becoming a Spiritual Pyromaniac

Connecting is a kind of relating that happens
when the powerful life of Christ in one person
meets the good life of Christ in another.
DR. LARRY CRABB

As a young boy I had a great fascination with fire. I loved to watch
things burn. So much so that at age five I managed to torch my entire
toy chest when the match I dropped into it set fire to a rubber rat, which
consequently set everything else on fire. As I recall, that pretty well put an
end to my pyromaniac activities. (Except for a slip-up a few years later
when I accidentally burned up a football field. But we won't go into that.)

One of the great purposes God has for our lives is to make us into
pyromaniacs. Spiritual ones, that is. We find this in the book of Hebrews:
"And let us consider one another in order to stir up love and good works,
not forsaking the assembling of ourselves together, as is the manner of
some, but exhorting one another, and so much the more as you see the
Day approaching" (Hebrews 10:24-25). The word used here for "stir up"
literally means to enflame or create a fever. One of the great purposes
for true community is to help enflame one another with a passion for
supernatural living—"stir up love and good works." It's much like what
our Lord did with the disciples on the Emmaus road: "Did not our

heart burn within us while He talked with us on the road, and while He opened the Scriptures to us?" (Luke 24:32). How then do we go about this divine calling?

The key word we find in this Hebrews 10 passage is *exhort*—"but exhorting one another." What does it mean to exhort? The word literally means to "call alongside." The noun form of the word is used by our Lord to describe the Holy Spirit as the "Helper"—literally, "the called alongside One" (see John 14:16). What are we "called alongside" to do? To help others fulfill their whole potential in Christ.

The concept of exhorting contains three central features, three different ways we can come alongside others to help stimulate godliness—to build up, to pull away, and to draw forth.

First, there's the building up, the encouraging aspect of exhorting. Pulling away is the warning aspect of exhorting. And drawing forth is the beckoning aspect of exhorting. All three are crucial; all have a necessary place. Like a pyramid, they're three sides of the same great enterprise.

We'll examine the warning and beckoning aspects in future chapters, but for now we'll focus on the encouraging side of helping others fulfill their whole potential in Christ—strengthening and nourishing the new nature. Like the wise gardener, we must know clearly what things to nourish and cultivate, as well as what to eradicate or leave alone.

This exhortation in Hebrews to "stir up" one another is based upon the realities of the New Covenant. In Hebrews 10:15-18, the writer quoted the great promise of the New Covenant from Jeremiah. He then gave the practical ramifications of these New Covenant promises in verses 19-25 (to draw near, to hold fast, to consider one another). But verse 19 begins with the significant connective word *therefore;* all the exhortations of verses 19-25 depend on the provisions of the New Covenant referred to in verses 15-18.

God is calling us to work with Him not to place fire into an empty box, but to ignite what He's already placed in the box. Within that box (our inner being) we've seen that Christ has placed four primary resources—a new purity, a new identity, a new disposition, and a new power. These are four aspects of the multifaceted work of the Holy Spirit in our hearts, or what Peter meant when he wrote that we've been made "partakers of the divine nature" (2 Peter 1:4).

In light of this, we want to explore how we can be used of God to strengthen, nourish, and even enflame these ever-present resources within every believer while we capitalize on our God-made differences.

To do this we'll look at words and actions in our relating with others that can help (1) highlight their new purity, (2) affirm their new identity, (3) arouse their new disposition, and (4) remind them of their new power. Again, this isn't intended to be a formula or technique for stimulating godliness. These are simply four areas we do well to keep in mind as we seek to be used of God in strengthening the inner selves of other believers. And it requires desperate dependence on the Holy Spirit for the wisdom and grace to know what to do or say in each situation.

THEIR NEW PURITY

Highlighting the new purity involves words and actions that draw attention to the new, God-wrought cleanness that clothes every believer from head to toe, and the implications this brings to daily living.

We find several examples of this in Scripture:

> And such were some of you. But you were washed, but you were sanctified, but you were justified in the name of the Lord Jesus and by the Spirit of our God. (1 Corinthians 6:11)

> Let us draw near with a true heart in full assurance of faith, having our hearts sprinkled from an evil conscience and our bodies washed with pure water. (Hebrews 10:22)

Since you have purified your souls in obeying the truth through the
Spirit in sincere love of the brethren, love one another fervently with
a pure heart, having been born again. (1 Peter 1:22-23)

Beloved, I now write to you this second epistle (in both of which I
stir up your pure minds by way of reminder). (2 Peter 3:1)

There are at least three good reasons for believers to highlight this
new purity.

Secure in Our Salvation

First, *it frees us from the tyranny of seeking to maintain or prove our salvation.*
The first thing we receive as believers is a vigorous assurance of salvation.
Before Paul began addressing sanctification in Romans, he laid its foundation by saying, "Therefore, having been justified by faith, we have peace
with God through our Lord Jesus Christ" (Romans 5:1). A deep-seated
assurance of our unalterable justification is the essential foundation for
properly building the house of sanctification. Without it, sanctification
can never occur the way God designed it to—by grace alone.

So many believers go through life seeking grimly to live for God in
order not to lose their salvation or to prove to God and themselves that
they're genuinely saved. Their hearts aren't set free to enjoy the exuberance
of unconditional acceptance. They fail to be released to worship and serve
God with a secure abandonment that has no questions whatsoever about
their standing with God.

Here are some of the questions I like to ask in helping others recognize and appreciate their new purity:

- When God looks down at you, what's the expression on His face?
- When God looks at you, what's He most aware of?
- When Christ died for your sins, did His blood cover all your sins
  or just most of them?

- If you did nothing to gain your salvation, what can you do to lose it?
- When God looks down at you, what's the first thing He sees?

It has been an unspeakable joy over the years to see the light come on in believers' eyes and joy light up their faces as I've pointed out to them from the Scriptures that God looks at them with eyes dancing with delight and a smile creasing His face, for He can't see us without seeing Jesus first. While He's aware of our sins, He's infinitely more aware of His perfect, gifted righteousness clothing us from head to toe. His blood covered all our trespasses, and therefore none can keep us from heaven. We did nothing to gain our salvation, and just as assuredly there's nothing we can do to lose our salvation. We have nothing left to prove to God. Jesus did it all.

Free from Guilt and Shame

The second reason to highlight the new purity is that *it frees us from the tyranny of pervading guilt and paralyzing shame.* One of Satan's primary tactics is to blanket us with an ongoing, pervasive sense of failure, guilt, and shame. This is different from the working of the Holy Spirit regarding sin in our lives, who always convicts in specifics. Isaiah cried out, "I am a man of unclean lips," when the holiness of God brought his sin to light (Isaiah 6:5). He didn't see his sin in generalities (oh, what a sinner I am), but specifically—"unclean lips." Charles Finney wrote, "The man who is convicted of one sin is convicted of all. But the man who is convicted of all sins is convicted of none."[1]

The darkness, heaviness, and despair that cripple so many believers' inner world has only one remedy—"having our hearts sprinkled from an evil conscience and our bodies washed with pure water" (Hebrews 10:22). Or in the words of Robert Lowry's hymn,

> What can wash away my sin? Nothing but the blood
> of Jesus;

> What can make me whole again? Nothing but the blood
>   of Jesus.
> Oh! Precious is the flow that makes me white as snow;
> No other fount I know, nothing but the blood of Jesus.[2]

Again, so many believers spend their days with a pervasive sense of internal griminess, though they know they're on their way to heaven. Yet the blood of Christ that saves us from the torments of hell is the same blood that saves us from the torments of conscience. Once confession has been made for revealed sin (see 1 John 1:9), then the exhilaration of a God-cleansed interior is God's will for every believer.

Some questions I've found helpful over the years are

- What else would you have to do to feel forgiven?
- What is God thinking about your sins right now?
- How white do you think God sees you?

One of the most valuable things we can do in supernaturally influencing others is *to make much of the blood of Christ.* Satan wants us to stay away from there at all costs. Why? Because it has such power to defeat him and his strategies. "They overcame [Satan] by the blood of the Lamb and by the word of their testimony, and they did not love their lives to the death" (Revelation 12:11).

Accepted As We Are

Still another reason to highlight the new purity is that *it frees us from the tyranny of trying to gain God's love.* The blood of Christ shouts once and for all on behalf of the Father, "I love you! There's nothing bad you can do to make Me love you less, and nothing good you can do to make Me love you more—it's impossible to love you more than I already do and always will."

All too many believers are living their lives under what they suppose to be God's frown or at least His keen sense of disappointment with them. In order to regain His love, they renew their commitment to Him, seeking to obey more fully. The reality is that God's love can't be increased or diminished. Perfect love is incapable of loving at varying degrees. While the expression of that love may vary (sometime His love is expressed through painful discipline), the presence and perfection of that love never wavers. "He made us accepted [literally, 'highly favored'] in the Beloved" (Ephesians 1:6).

Where do we look to find out how deeply God loves us? The cross. Where do we look to find out how fully God loves us? The cross. Where do we look to find out how unconditionally God loves us? Again, the cross. "To Him who loved us and washed us from our sins in His blood..." (Revelation 1:5).

Some questions that might be helpful here:

- What do you need to do for God to love you more?
- What things are you looking for to let you know God still loves you?
- What would be the one thing that could convince you of God's love?

Our new purity reminds us that the love we so desperately thirst for, the love we were created for, the love without which we unravel—this same love is unwaveringly and incalculably ours once we're in the Beloved. What joy to be the bearers of news like that!

THEIR NEW IDENTITY

The next resource we want to emphasize in our encouragement of believers is their new identity. This involves words and actions that assert their new, God-crafted personal uniqueness and its implications for daily living.

Again, we see this often in the Scriptures:

And such were some of you. But you were washed, but you were
sanctified. (1 Corinthians 6:11)

Or do you not know that your body is the temple of the Holy Spirit?
(1 Corinthians 6:19)

Clearly you are an epistle of Christ. (2 Corinthians 3:3)

For you died, and your life is hidden with Christ in God. When
Christ who is our life appears, then you also will appear with Him
in glory. (Colossians 3:3-4)

One of the most effective ways we can help believers is in carefully distinguishing their new identity from their flesh and affirming that identity.
The writers of Scripture did this again and again. Paul rebuked the carnal
Corinthian believers for their sexual immorality, using their true identity
as his rallying point. "And such were some of you.... Do you not know
that your body is the temple of the Holy Spirit?" (1 Corinthians 6:11,19).
Paul never addressed believers as sinners needing to shape up, but as saints
needing to give in—to their new, Christ-united identity.

What are some of the ways we can do the same thing?

Be careful with "you are" statements. Whenever we use that phrase we're
targeting identity, and our flesh never defines who we truly are as believers.

I try to be careful never to say to a believer, "You're a workaholic" or
"You're a sex addict" or "You're a manipulator." Instead, we could say, "It
seems to me that you have a significant problem with sexual addiction, yet
I know that deep down you want to be free of it."

I spoke with a young woman recently who recalled the day her doctor
told her, "The tests show that you are bipolar." That statement shattered
her world because to her it defined her fundamental identity. She no longer
saw herself as a disciple of Jesus Christ struggling with some depression

issues, but as a mentally unstable woman who happened to also be a Christian. See the difference?

It was my joy to let her know that she was not bipolar. She was a daughter of the King, a new creation in Christ, a partaker of the divine nature, a disciple of Jesus Christ. That didn't mean she should stop taking her medication, but that her bipolar struggles had nothing to do with who she really was. I wish you could have been there to see the new light in her countenance and see the tears fill her eyes and at the end to almost shout, "This captive has been set free!" Identity is an incredibly powerful issue, for better or for worse. Through the Spirit of God we can be used to help other saints lock on to who they really are in Christ.

Be careful also with "you always" or "you never." These come close to causing the same problem as "you are" statements.

A better way to attack sin without attacking identity is to say, "That was out of character for you" or "This is where your flesh is showing." I have a good friend who has said this to me on more than one occasion. I find it much easier to hear his rebuke because I don't feel my identity threatened.

One of the greatest gifts we can have in life is friends who can say something like, "There's such a beauty (or strength) in you that has yet to be fully released." They see in us what we don't see in ourselves, and they envision for us what God can do through us.

This, too, is a major part of our divine job description as supernatural influencers. God has called all of us to be of the offspring of Barnabas, sons and daughters of encouragement.

This is more than a calling; it's an internal compulsion placed within us by the Spirit of God who is so rightly described by Jesus as "the Helper." One of the greatest ways people are spiritually helped is through sincere and honest expressions of encouragement. "Pleasant words are like a honeycomb," Solomon wrote, "sweetness to the soul and health to the bones" (Proverbs 16:24).

People are dying for encouragement. Mark Twain said, "I can live for two months on a good compliment." Think of the times in your life when someone deeply encouraged you. Aren't these some of your fondest memories and often pivotal experiences for moving forward?

When Abraham Lincoln's pockets were emptied after his assassination, one of the things discovered was a well-worn newspaper clipping he'd carried around for months. It was an article describing him as a great leader. One can only imagine how much those words must have meant at that juncture of his life and how often he must have reread them. What power words of affirmation can have!

What we aren't talking about here is flattery or self-serving complimenting of others. That's the fleshly counterfeit of the real thing. Truly, Spirit-wrought encouragement is utterly centered on benefiting the other person for the glory of God.

An unusual joy comes from humbling ourselves enough to become passionate encouragers of others. Many of us are passive encouragers, occasionally passing on compliments when it seems appropriate. But it requires the Spirit of God to become a passionate encourager, one who's actively on the lookout for how to be a Barnabas in others' lives. Such encouragement—affirming others' identity in Christ and the work of God in their lives—is one of the most central ministries of the Spirit through us. And the wider our floodgates are opened, the greater the joy we experience.

Their New Disposition

In addition to highlighting their new purity and new identity, we want to arouse the new disposition of other believers through words and actions that help stir up and enflame their new, supernatural appetite for God and His ways, an appetite that was given all of us at our conversion.

Again, we find several examples of this in Scripture.

Did not our heart burn within us while He talked with us on the road? (Luke 24:32)

And let us consider one another in order to stir up love and good works. (Hebrews 10:24)

I think it is right, as long as I am in this tent, to stir you up by reminding you. (2 Peter 1:13)

One of the greatest paradigm shifts in my Christian life was the discovery that God has caused every believer to want to do His will at the deepest level of their being. This is what is meant by the promise of the New Covenant: "I will put My laws into their hearts, and in their minds I will write them" (Hebrews 10:16).

Our calling isn't to shame or coerce believers into doing what they don't want to, but to help them enjoy and appropriate what God is already urging them toward through His indwelling Spirit. Here are some questions or statements I've found helpful, and my thoughts on each one:

What Do You Really Want?

Often the only longing they seem aware of is the desire of their flesh. But when people take some time to ponder what they really want, it helps them get beneath the flesh to the new nature.

I was once talking with a lady going through extreme marriage difficulties. I asked her what she wanted. Vehemently she replied, "I want a divorce." "Okay," I responded, "now think for a moment and tell me what you really want." She thought for a moment, then with tears streaming down her eyes she said, "What I really want is for my husband to love me." She'd gotten past her flesh to her new nature.

Did That Feel Clean?

A good friend of mine asked me that question one night as we were discussing a particular story I'd told that afternoon while speaking at a conference. I thought it was a great question, and it has always stuck with me. Fortunately, on that occasion I was able to answer yes. But there have certainly been other times when I honestly couldn't say that.

One of the best ways I can tell whether I'm operating out of the flesh or if the Spirit of God is being allowed to flow through me is an internal sense of cleanness. This is particularly true in evaluating my motives. Since in this life we'll never have absolutely pure motives, the vital question is this: What is our controlling or dominating motive? When my motive springs mostly from the flesh (ego, greed, sensuality), I never feel clean on the inside. But when the Spirit has primary sway, I experience an internal sense of flowing purity. In those times we can personally affirm with David, "The fear of the LORD is clean" (Psalm 19:9).

It's certainly true that believers can harden their hearts, quench the Spirit, and lose sense of the experiential reality of the indwelling Spirit. But on the whole, when believers are walking in the light, we can count on the reality that the Spirit of God within them will confirm His pleasure in what they're doing through a sense of interior cleanness. Likewise, when they're walking in darkness, this same Spirit will express His grief (see Ephesians 4:30) by withdrawing that sense of cleanness and letting them taste the dirt of pigpen living.

Did You Find Joy in That?

This is closely tied to the issue of cleanness. When the Spirit is flowing through our lives, we experience not only a relaxed strength and internal cleanness but also a joy, though the level of this joy may vary dramatically. We'll still face the reality of those dark nights of the soul and the times of feeling abandoned by God, just as Jesus did. These, too, are a part of walking with God, so the absence of joy may not necessarily mean we aren't keeping in step with the Spirit. It may be that the Spirit has led us into a valley where, like our Lord, we become men and women "of sorrows and acquainted with grief" (Isaiah 53:3).

But on the whole, when the Spirit is moving through us, we feel some sense of joy (as distinguished from mere happiness or pleasure). Even from prison Paul could write, "If I am being poured out as a drink offering on the sacrifice and service of your faith, I am glad and rejoice with you all" (Philippians 2:17).

We can bank on the fact, once again, that when a believer is walking in the light, the Spirit of God will confirm His pleasure through an interior sense of joy, though the outside circumstances may also bring an ache to their heart and tears to their eyes (see 1 Peter 1:6-8). We also can know that God will not allow His joy to be tasted while this same believer is dining at other tables.

When Do You Feel Most Alive As a Man (or Woman)?

The Spirit of God is going to reflect Christlikeness differently through a man than through a woman. (On this crucial topic, I highly recommend Larry Crabb's book *Men and Women: Enjoying the Difference*.)

What Do You Most Enjoy in Ministry?

A unique, Spirit-imparted passion comes from serving God in the right place, through the right gifting, by the right power, and for the right reasons. I call it hitting the bull's-eye. When we're doing the will of God through the gift of God by the Spirit of God for the glory of God, we normally experience a kind of holy fire from within.

I think this is what Paul was alluding to when he told Timothy to "kindle afresh the gift of God which is in you" (2 Timothy 1:6, NASB). It's the deep and humble sense of satisfaction that Jesus was referring to when

He said, "My food is to do the will of Him who sent Me, and to finish His work" (John 4:34). His working with God was tiring at times, but it also was deeply satisfying, as food for the hungry heart.

I encourage believers to pay attention to their passion. When you're involved in ministry, what kinds of things resonate most deeply within? What activities leave you energized rather than drained? Especially, is there anything in particular you do that causes something within you to whisper, *Yes, this is what I was made for*.

A friend of mine named Gil serves with Wycliffe Bible Translators in computer support. He told me not long ago about an incident when he was up in the mountains of Peru helping a translator whose computer had crashed. He said he was working away on this computer, sitting outside in great heat with flies and mosquitoes buzzing all around him. In the middle of it all, he said he became so overwhelmed by the depth of joy and satisfaction he was experiencing in helping fix this translator's computer that he leaned back in his chair, stretched out his arms, and almost shouted, "*This* is what I was made for!"

I personally find this in speaking and writing. My wife finds it in meeting with individuals who are willing to be honest with their lives and their walk with God. Others find it in evangelizing, while others in helping quietly behind the scenes. Central to recognizing your spiritual gift is recognizing the accompanying passion God gives when you use it.

These are just a few examples of questions and ways God might use you in helping arouse the new disposition He has placed in all believers. They're only tools, and at all times they depend upon the grace and wisdom of the Holy Spirit to be used effectively.

THEIR NEW POWER

In addition to the other three resources present within a believer's life, we want to remind them of their new power through words and actions that help take their eyes off their own weakness and to focus instead on Christ's strength.

Scripture is replete with examples of this:

Fear not, for I am with you;
Be not dismayed, for I am your God.
I will strengthen you,
Yes, I will help you,
I will uphold you with My righteous right hand.
      (Isaiah 41:10)

"Not by might nor by power, but by My Spirit,"
Says the LORD of Hosts. (Zechariah 4:6)

But we have this treasure in earthen vessels, that the excellence
of the power may be of God and not of us. (2 Corinthians 4:7)

For God has not given us a spirit of fear, but of power and of love
and of a sound mind. (2 Timothy 1:7)

One of the greatest mistakes we make in influencing others is an overemphasis on responsibilities and an underemphasis on resource. I like to tell Christian workers, "Be heavier on resource than you are on responsibility." We don't back away from or diminish biblical responsibility, but we would have far greater impact if we would sandwich it between two slices of resource. The resource is where the hope for responsibility lies. Following are some examples of how we communicate this:

"I'm Excited to See What God Is Going to Do Through You."
This is one of the ways my wife most encourages me. She's not excited to see what I'm going to do, and rightly so! But God has used her so much

over the years to help me believe in what God can do through me if I'll give Him the chance.

"God Will Never Call You to Something You Can Do. He'll Call You Only to That Which Requires Him."
I said this recently during a chapel message at a seminary, then fleshed out what I meant by it. Afterward, a professor came up to me with tears in his eyes. He shared how utterly overwhelmed he felt by his responsibilities and that he had lost all hope. God used that simple thought to draw the man's focus back to Himself, to see that his only true hope was the God who wanted to do the work through him in the first place.

"You Don't Have What It Takes, and You Never Will—but God Does!"

Or ask this question:

"Where Do You Sense the Greatest Need for God's Power Right Now?"

LET GOD'S WORDS FLOW THROUGH YOU

These are just examples of what to say or ask. The most important thing is to depend radically on God for the right words at the right time, and to speak them in the right manner for the right purpose. Ministry done properly is always done supernaturally. God never calls us to something we can do on our own.

These four arenas of divine resourcing—a new purity, a new identity, a new disposition, and a new power—are at the heart of what it means to strengthen and nourish the new nature. They're central to building up and encouraging others. But they must not be viewed in any sense as mechanical or formulaic. The guidelines in this chapter are mere suggestions and have no power in and of themselves. Ask God to show you personally how you can become His conduit for enflaming others to love and good works.

One final word: If you find all this material cumbersome and difficult to hold on to, especially when actually ministering to others, then drop it all for one simple goal—be an encourager! Be a passionate encourager! Don't worry about all the intricacies of the four provisions; just avail yourself to God and allow His voice of encouragement to use your vocal cords for the time being. Let His hug for another come through your arms. Let His smile for your friend be formed through your lips. And most of all, let His unrivaled love for the person before you flow through your heart to theirs.

Pulling the Weeds

Sin is the suicidal abandonment of joy.

JOHN PIPER

One summer in my college years, during a tennis tournament in Montgomery, Alabama, I was fortunate enough to be given housing with a Dr. Yow and his wonderful, gracious family.

One rainy afternoon I went down to the local YMCA to get some exercise by playing a few games of pick-up basketball. All was going well until I tried to steal the ball from the guy I was guarding. As I reached around him, he swirled in the opposite direction. My nose collided with his right elbow. I felt as if my face had just exploded.

Immediately, I went to the locker room to survey the damage. Blood was streaming down my face, and my nose had a new thirty-degree bend to it. I knew this meant I probably had a broken nose. And the remedy for broken noses was one I really didn't care for.

As I looked in the mirror I thought, *My nose has never been much of an asset to my looks anyway. It really won't make that much difference to leave it the way it is.*

Late that afternoon I was back at the Yows' home, relaxing and drinking tea with the family on their back porch. When Dr. Yow returned from work, he took one look at me and said, "Let's go." He drove me straight to the emergency room of the hospital where he worked and stayed with me while another doctor (whose name I'm pretty sure was Igor) came and examined my nose.

Igor put his fingers on both sides of my nose and said, "If this hurts too bad, let me know." Before I could say anything he snapped my nose back into place. Before I could scream it was over. My nose was back in place, though not by a method I would ever have chosen.

I'll always be grateful to Dr. Yow for caring enough about me to get my nose straightened out (though it still isn't much of an asset to my looks) when I would never have chosen it on my own.

Spiritually speaking, we're all walking around with broken noses and fractured legs. While we're most assuredly new creations in Christ, our daily practice hasn't yet caught up with our eternal personhood. Left to ourselves, we would often continue to live with our broken noses and disjointed limbs. Blessed are those who have friends who love them enough not just to praise the good but also reset the broken.

This is the imagery behind Galatians 6:1—"Brethren, if a man is overtaken in any trespass, you who are spiritual restore such a one in a spirit of gentleness, considering yourself lest you also be tempted." The word for "restore" was often used in that day of a doctor resetting a broken bone. Paul's words call on us to humbly involve ourselves in the spiritual repair of saints who are temporarily fractured by sin. As in resetting a bone, this is to be done as gently as possible, but also as firmly as necessary. Difficult as this may be at times, it's another key aspect of being a supernatural influencer.

EXPOSING SIN'S PERVERSITY AND INSANITY

Having looked at what it means to strengthen and nourish the new nature, we now want to explore what it means to expose the perversity and insanity of sin so that we can "reset the broken bones." Using our gardening illustration, we'll focus now on the things that need to be confronted and eliminated—and how to pull these weeds. Or in our three-sided understanding of the word *exhort,* this is the side of "pulling away" or warning.

The prophet Jeremiah was given this as an integral part of his ministry. God told him, "See, I have this day set you over the nations and over the kingdoms, to root out and to pull down, to destroy and to throw down, to build and to plant" (Jeremiah 1:10). His ministry was to both pull weeds and plant flowers. So is ours, if we're to have supernatural influence.

By "pulling weeds" I mean cooperating with God in exposing the perversity and insanity of sin. Actually, we can never pull up the weed for someone else; that can be done only between God and the individual. But we can be used by God to soften the soil and break up the dirt.

It's a grave misconception that living under grace somehow downgrades the need for obedience or leads us to be soft on sin. Grace sees sin through the lenses of divine love, and this love is never willing to overlook cancer just so the patient won't be inconvenienced. Due to its depth and genuineness, in fact, this love can't bear to leave the infection untreated.

In this chapter we'll look at what sin is, why it's both wrong and foolish, and how to expose it. Again, my intent isn't to give a formula or techniques, but tools that the Holy Spirit can use as He works through us to bring about genuine conviction.

It's crucial to gain a clear picture of what sin is, lest we pull up more than weeds in our spiritual gardening or miss pulling all the weeds. Sin involves both internal disposition and external actions. As A. W. Tozer said, "Sins are because sin is."[1] Paul quoted from the Psalms to remind us, "There is none righteous, no, not one.... There is none who does good, no, not one" (Romans 3:10-12).

We're born into this world hostile toward God in our fallen nature. "The carnal mind is enmity against God; for it is not subject to the law of God, nor indeed can be" (Romans 8:7). This part of us, the flesh, is never upgraded or improved over time. It may find more respectable and refined ways to express its God-defiance, but it will never be diminished or eradicated until heaven. This hostile nature exhibits itself in concrete actions of spiritual rebellion, though these actions may be well camouflaged in religious or humanitarian clothing.

The following definitions of sin can help us see the weeds properly.

Sin Is Taking a God-Given Longing and Going in a God-Absent Direction

God says, "My people have committed two evils: they have forsaken Me, the fountain of living waters, and hewn themselves cisterns—broken cisterns that can hold no water" (Jeremiah 2:13). The Israelites had taken the legitimate thirst God placed within them and sought to quench it at watering holes that contained nothing of God.

Ultimately, *sin is always mismanagement of something good*. It's taking our God-implanted hunger and thirst to tables and fountains that can't do the job they boast of. They'll never satisfy us. Sin, as Augustine said, is "energy in the wrong channel."

In helping others (as well as ourselves) to deal with sin, it's valuable to recognize what it is we really thirst and hunger for. We thirst for a love that can't be lost or even diminished by our performance. We hunger to make an impact in life that can't fade or be erased over time. These heart-cries within each of us are incredibly strong, for the simple reason that God placed them there.

As we help others with their sin issues, it's critical that we give them something more than admonitions to stay away from the wrong things. That's like telling a famished man not to eat junk food. We must show them the legitimate, God-catered banquet and encourage them to feast unreservedly there. John Eldredge, in commenting on what happens too often today, wrote, "What we have left is a Christianity of tips and techniques.... It does not take your breath away, and if Christianity does not take your breath away, something else will."[2] One of our greatest ministries in others' lives is to personally model and lovingly remind of the best Place to go for having one's breath taken away.

Sin Is Always Rooted in Unbelief

"When He [the Holy Spirit] has come, He will convict the world of sin, and of righteousness, and of judgment: of sin, because they do not believe in Me" (John 16:8-9). This passage led Luther to assert that the root of all sin is unbelief—unbelief in God's goodness, unbelief in His power, unbelief in His faithfulness, and on and on.

We find this going all the way back to the garden. In Genesis 3, what was Satan's strategy in getting the man and woman to eat from the tree?

- Unbelief in God's *infallible Word.* Satan began his questioning of Eve with the words, "Has God indeed said…?" (3:1).
- Unbelief in God's *overwhelming goodness.* Satan put these words in God's mouth: "You shall not eat of every tree in the garden" (3:1). But God placed only one tree off-limits. Satan always seeks to exaggerate God's strictness.
- Unbelief in God's *certain judgment:* "You will not surely die," Satan insisted (3:4).
- Unbelief in God's *unrivaled supremacy:* "You will be like God," Satan said, "knowing good and evil" (3:5).

At every turn the devil attacked Eve's faith in her Creator. Perhaps this is one reason faith means so much to God. It's our in-your-face response to Satan's "You're a fool to trust this God."

One area in which this understanding of sin becomes so important is the issue of repentance. What is repentance? What exactly are we calling saints to repent of? Most commonly we think of repentance as a change of behavior, but the New Testament word translated as "repent" *(metanoeo)* means "to change the mind." Repentance, properly understood, is a change in our thinking on the issue of *where life is found.* When this mind-change happens, a change in actions inevitably will follow. But it's possible to change our actions without really changing our mind. In a real sense, it's possible to repent without repenting.

We all know that if you pull up a weed without extracting its roots at the same time, it's just a matter of time until the weed comes back. In the same way, if we try to get people to change their actions without helping them understand the belief system motivating those actions, it's only a matter of time until the actions manifest themselves again, though sometimes in different ways.

Paul therefore tells us to be transformed "by the renewing of your mind" (Romans 12:2), not by changing our practices.

I spoke recently with a young man who candidly admitted to a struggle with cheating on tests. How would you try to help him? So often, we begin by thinking through specific helpful actions—get an accountability partner, memorize verses, and so on. But over the years, I've found that a helpful rule is to first explore the belief system behind the practice before trying to change the practice. Always begin by asking, "In order to do such a thing, where does this person believe life is found?"

As we chatted I discovered he was feeling immense pressure from his parents to achieve a high level of academic success, beyond what he thought he could produce. The root issue for him really didn't have to do with dishonesty, but with a tenaciously held belief that life was found in his parents' approval. Until he could see that his greatest sin lay with the idolatry of finding life in his parents' approval, no alteration of external circumstances would have an adequate or lasting effect on the issue of cheating.

Sin Is Failure to Glorify God

"For all have sinned and fall short of the glory of God" (Romans 3:23). The fundamental meaning of the word translated here as "sinned" is "to miss the mark." We see that so clearly here. Sin is missing the mark of what matters most to God—His glory.

Sin runs much deeper and wider than we normally take into account.

How many times during the day do we steal, lie, murder, or commit adultery? Hopefully very few, if at all. Yet how many times do we fail to glorify God? Clearly that's a different story.

Understanding this will help keep us from downgrading sin's standard. The propensity of our flesh is to always pick a standard that we measure up favorably against and use it to determine our godliness. Am I a good basketball player? It all depends on the standard. Compared to my sons who rarely play, yes. Compared to Michael Jordan, obviously no.

Listen to the standard of the Pharisee in Luke 18. "God, I thank You that I am not like other men—extortioners, unjust, adulterers, or even as this tax collector" (18:11). Look at his standard, the people he carefully selected to measure himself against so that he might elevate himself. Yet he was far more like these people than he knew or wanted to know.

When we begin to think of sin as our failure to glorify God in any area of life, at any point, at any time, for any reason, then it throws us back onto our overwhelming neediness for God during every nanosecond of the day. The primary purpose God has in showing us our failure is not to make us feel bad, but to make us feel desperate. To live as He has called us to live—not just staying away from bad things, but flaunting His spectacularness in whatever setting He places us—requires a passionate neediness that too few of us have deeply tasted. The reason may well be that we've set the bar far too low.

How We Deflect Our Guilt

One of Satan's unwavering tactics is to get us to see sin as only a personal weakness, an excusable slip-up. To the degree we give in to this perspective, we'll fail to appreciate the gravity of what we've done. We fail to see sin's wickedness, its true perversity.

But even after we start sensing the evil we've done, our flesh has four primary ways of deflecting the true moral guilt that we experience through sin.

Dismissal

We try to forget about it and keep it at bay through focusing on other things. It's what David tried when he wrote, "When I kept silent, my bones grew old through my groaning all the day long" (Psalm 32:3). The problem is that while the mind may be able to preoccupy itself with other things, the conscience has nowhere to turn for quiet and peace.

Blame-Shifting

This was man's first response to his true moral guilt. "The woman whom You gave to be with me, she gave me of the tree, and I ate" (Genesis 3:12). He was complaining, "It was your fault, God, for giving me the woman in the first place, and it was her fault for giving me fruit from the tree."

This is undoubtedly man's most common way of dealing with guilt. We blame the sin in our lives on the dysfunctionality of the home we grew up in, the personality temperament we were born with, the actions of those around us—on anything but ourselves. Jeremiah captured the situation well: "No man repented of his wickedness, saying, 'What have *I* done?'" (Jeremiah 8:6). Yet, try as we may to cast our blame onto others, our conscience can't be pacified by this rerouting of our true moral guilt.

Rationalization

Here we seek to minimize our sin by heightening its reasonableness. This is seen in Saul's response to Samuel concerning why he had sinned in offering the sacrifice. "When I saw that the people were scattered…and that you did not come…and that the Philistines gathered together…I felt compelled, and offered a burnt offering" (1 Samuel 13:11-12). There's always a good reason for sin, but never a good enough one. Highlighting its reasonableness still can't dislodge its accusations within our breast.

Another way the flesh seeks to rationalize sin is to rename it. This is done in the vain hope that a nicer, newer label will muffle the cry of guilt in the soul. Thus sin is now called "an alternate lifestyle," "a genetic predisposition," "a midlife crisis," or "a personality weakness." Again, the problem is that while the mind can play all the word games it wants, guilt in the conscience is never removed by a mere label change.

Penance

This is man's way of personally repaying the wrong he has done, believing that denial or punishment of self will quiet the guilt he feels. "Even though you make many prayers, I will not hear. Your hands are full of blood" (Isaiah 1:15). Even something as good as prayer can be used as an attempt to make up for sin in our life. No denial of self or personal sacrifice has anywhere near the merit needed to cleanse our conscience of personal guilt.

As long as people yawn at their sin, excuse their sin, relabel their sin, or try to pay God back for their sin, genuine repentance can never take place. Without recognizing the awfulness of our sin there cannot be the sorrow that leads to repentance (see 2 Corinthians 7:8-11).

The starting point for genuine repentance is the full and unreserved embracing of the wickedness of our sin. Wicked because of the damage it has done to others. Wicked because of the damage it has done to us. But most of all, wicked because of the damage it has done to God's name. The greatest heinousness in sin is that the glory of God is obscured for the time being and His reputation is tarnished. After the children of Israel had made a golden calf for themselves, Moses burned the idol "and ground it to powder; and he scattered it on the water and made the children of Israel drink it" (Exodus 32:20). How do you suppose the water tasted? Bitter, to say the least. In a similar fashion, God's design is that we taste, through the convicting work of the Holy Spirit, the bitterness of idolatry—as a vivid reminder of where life is not found.

I used to think and teach that the most important thing to recognize about sin is how foolish it is. But I've come to appreciate more and more through my own life, through the lives of others, and especially from the Scriptures, that there's a crucial place for godly shame. In Jeremiah's day,

God's indictment on the people when they "committed abomination" was that "they were not at all ashamed, nor did they know how to blush" (Jeremiah 6:15; 8:12). Through the prophet Joel, the Lord calls out, "Turn to Me with all your heart, with fasting, with weeping, and with mourning. So rend your heart, and not your garments" (Joel 2:12-13). James called on those who were spiritual adulterers (and that's each of us, at some point) to "lament and mourn and weep! Let your laughter be turned to mourning and your joy to gloom" (James 4:9). Paul spoke of a "godly sorrow...not to be regretted" (2 Corinthians 7:10).

Too many of us (and I include myself) can't remember the last time we were brought to tears by our sin (if ever). Yet there's something about fully embracing the hot shame of the wickedness and heinousness of our high treason against God in defying His ways that makes the blood of Christ all the more precious and the Spirit of God all the more necessary, lest we immediately fall back again.

WHY SIN IS INSANE

Sin, however, is not just wrong for the believer; it's also *foolish.* "O foolish Galatians!... Are you so foolish?" (Galatians 3:1-3). It seems to me that until a believer understands that his sin is just as foolish as it is wrong, he'll probably not change.

Why is sin insanity for believers? For at least two main reasons.

The first is that *who we really are militates against sin.* As new creations in Christ we have an unalterable new identity, one that was made for supernatural righteousness. "What shall we say then? Shall we continue in sin that grace may abound? Certainly not! How shall we who died to sin live any longer in it?" (Romans 6:1-2). In fact the whole of Romans 6 is an expansion of Paul's incredulity that Christians would even entertain the thought of continuing to live in sin, given the radical new persons they had become through conversion.

It's as if we were street dwellers, eating leftovers out of trash cans for our survival. Then one day a wealthy and kind gentleman takes pity on us and invites us to come be part of his family. We're fed at his table, clothed by his money. What would he think if he went out one day, and as he was driving around, he saw us sifting through the trash cans again for something to eat? How insane for us to go back to these provisions when he'd seen to it that everything we needed was amply taken care of. Yet when we go back into sin, this is exactly what we do. It's not just wrong, it's incredibly foolish.

When Paul addressed sin in believers' lives, he often began with the question, "Do you not know…?" (Romans 6:3,16; 1 Corinthians 6:2-3,9,15,19). It's as if he was saying, "If you'll stop and remember who you really are now that you're a new creation in Christ, you'll see the path you're heading on is sheer lunacy. What are you thinking? Your new design is never going to change to allow you to be satisfied with sin; you'll be incessantly swimming upstream against its divine current. Why not just give in and allow yourself to be swept along in the only current you're made for—that of supernatural righteousness?"

The second reason sin is insanity for us is that *we can never have the satisfaction we long for in sin.* In case you hadn't noticed, becoming a Christian really messes up sin. When we trust Christ, God places a bent in our soul that can never be straightened. That bent is delight in and commitment toward the righteousness of God. "And if Christ is in you, the body is dead because of sin, but the Spirit is life because of righteousness" (Romans 8:10).

Believers can live in defiance of that bent, but they can never alter it. That's why the believer living in sin is really the most miserable creature on earth. He can't get the divine bent of his soul taken away, yet that bent robs him of the ability to fully enjoy sin. He knows at the deepest level of his being that he was made for God, and his rebellion against righteousness is an ongoing kicking against the goads.

Meanwhile, living as out-and-out disciples of Christ is the greatest favor believers can do for themselves on this earth. It means falling in line with their God-crafted design. When is an eagle most satisfied—in a cage or out in nature? Obviously out in nature because it was created by God to soar high above the earth. Likewise, no believer can be fully satisfied while caged in sin. We were made to soar, to feel the currents of God's Spirit under our wings, moving us to ever-increasing heights of godliness. This is the vibrant rest our souls were made for. Why trade it for this world's peanuts?

Keeping Them on Their Horses

Having seen the perversity and insanity of living by the old nature, how can we be used of God to help influence others to deal with their weeds? Again, there's no easy answer, but let me suggest three things:

First and foremost, *model the joy of radical weed extraction ourselves.* Nothing speaks louder or more convincingly than example. "Let no one despise your youth, but be an example to the believers in word, in conduct, in love, in spirit, in faith, in purity...that your progress may be evident to all" (1 Timothy 4:12,15). As others see us running alongside them, pulling many of the same weeds they need to be pulling, and doing so not morbidly or self-righteously, but with supernatural joy and vibrancy, this will set the stage for the greatest opportunity for impact.

Second, *utilize stories and illustrations.* This was how Nathan so powerfully confronted David (see 2 Samuel 12:1-15). As you read in the New Testament, you'll notice that nearly every time Jesus spoke, He used an illustration of some kind (see Mark 4:34). We all think in pictures, and a story or illustration often can communicate the perversity and insanity of sin in penetrating ways. We see this countless times in the Scriptures.

And third, *focus on both God-given longings and God-resistant strategies.* We're to keep both in mind as we work with others. Ask God to show you how to remind them of their deep-seated longings and to affirm their goodness and importance. Ask also how to expose the sinful strategies that dishonor God and rob them of what they really want most.

Clarence Macartney tells about a friend of General Ulysses S. Grant who had an exemplary ability to warn as well as to encourage:

> General Grant's chief of staff, the Galena lawyer John A. Rawlins, was closer to Grant than any other during the war. It was to Rawlins that Grant gave his pledge that he would abstain from intoxicating liquors. When he broke that pledge Rawlins went to him and with great earnestness pleaded with him, for the sake of himself and for the sake of the great holy cause of the nation, to refrain from strong drink. Faithful were the wounds of a friend. In front of the Capitol at Washington today there stands the magnificent monument of General Grant, sitting on his horse in characteristic pose and flanked on either side by stirring battle scenes. But at the other end of Pennsylvania Avenue, a little to the south of the avenue, is Rawlins Park, where there stands a very commonplace statue of Rawlins. Whenever I stand before the great monument of Grant on his horse there in front of the Capitol, I think of that other monument. I think of that faithful friend who kept Grant on his horse.[3]

One of our highest callings and privileges is to become a spiritual Rawlins—someone who through the grace and wisdom of the Spirit can help keep other believers on their horses. Sometimes this means passionate encouragement; at other times, strong warning. But always it means desperate dependence on the flow of God through us for any hope of lasting influence.

Now, what is it that we're helping other saints stay on horseback for?

Divine Credentials

The world is not going to pay much attention
to all the organized efforts of the Christian church.
The one thing she will pay attention to is a body
of believers filled with a spirit of rejoicing.

MARTYN LLOYD-JONES

One day when I was five years old and playing in our front yard with my younger brother (age four), we somehow came up with the brilliant idea to throw rocks at passing cars. This went on for a while—our aim wasn't good enough to actually hit one. Then finally my brother connected. And the car came to a screeching halt.

Before we could think of how to get away, a large man got out of his vehicle and came over to us. He asked who had thrown the rock.

My brother admitted it and apologized, saying he was really sorry.

But this didn't seem to appease the man. He kept bawling us out, until I finally decided to speak up. "Listen, mister, my brother said he's sorry. What more do you want?"

The man glared at me. "Son, do you know who I am?"

"No sir," I replied.

He took out his wallet, opened it, and showed us a large badge inside it. My brother had managed to hit an unmarked police car!

My attitude changed immediately. I realized I'd better take this man seriously—especially when the man asked if we wanted to call our parents from jail or from the house.

We were both shaking. Finally he let us go with a stern lecture and a promise from us that we would never throw rocks at cars again. And we never did.

God wants to use you and me to do the same thing that policeman did with his badge. God wants us to be the credentials He holds out to a dark and unbelieving world.

Paul wrote, "Clearly you are an epistle of Christ, ministered by us, written not with ink but by the Spirit of the living God" (2 Corinthians 3:3). The image here is of "letters of commendation" (3:1), something much like a diploma. Through the resources of the New Covenant, our lives can actually serve as letters of commendation for God—living, breathing reasons why people should take God seriously. What an honor! What a calling! What an utter impossibility apart from the Spirit of the living God!

To this end we seek to keep other believers on their horses—not for what they can do for us or our ministry, but what they can do for God. And we have the high privilege of being used by God to shape the kinds of credentials that can potentially stop people in their tracks and cause them to give due regard to the Sovereign of the universe.

BECKONING THEM TO JOY

We now turn to the last aspect of supernaturally influencing others: beckoning them to a more God-honoring and personally satisfying plane of living. Drawing believers to the calling that overshadows all other callings and to the joy that outstrips all other joys—to be more like Jesus. This is the third side of our understanding of the word *exhort*. We've seen that this great word means "to call alongside." Sometimes it means to call alongside for the purpose of encouraging and building up. Other times it means to call alongside for the purpose of warning and helping pull away. Here we're going to see that this calling alongside is also for the purpose of beckoning and drawing forth. In our garden imagery, this is the joyous exhibiting of the flowers, the end result of all the other activities.

Everything we've looked at so far has been leading up to this. The goal of supernaturally influencing others is to cooperate with God in seeing His colors put unmistakably on display through their lives. Whether we're desiring to influence our children, our spouse, or our Christian friends, nothing is more important than one overriding question: What are they doing for God's reputation on earth? Nothing matters more than this, because nothing matters more than God. Period.

This God-drenched view of life and people is at the heart of the New Covenant, for in promising that covenant God said, "I do not do this for your sake...but for My holy name's sake" (Ezekiel 36:22).

It's also at the heart of our daily activities: "Therefore, whether you eat or drink, or whatever you do, do all to the glory of God" (1 Corinthians 10:31). It's at the heart of why we have children and what we raise them for: "He seeks godly offspring" (Malachi 2:15). It's at the heart of doing evangelism: "that grace, having spread through the many, may cause thanksgiving to abound to the glory of God" (2 Corinthians 4:15). And it's at the heart of why we do ministry: "As each one has received a gift, minister it to one another...that in all things God may be glorified through Jesus Christ" (1 Peter 4:10-11).

God hasn't called us to work with Him in producing safe, predictable, clean-living, rule-keeping, Bible-toting moralists. He's already got way too many of them as it is. What He's seeking to use us for is in helping mold Spirit-dependent, Christ-enamored men and women who honor Him. Something about their lives elevates other people's respect and regard of *Him.* There's an undeniable surprise element in the way these saints relate and persevere that defies being quickly or easily explained away—that trilogy of a joy that can't be explained, a peace that can't be sabotaged, and a love that can't be imitated.

The beauty of it all is that as we beckon believers to this kind of irrepressible, Christ-exuding way of life, we're simultaneously inviting them to taste the kind of joy and satisfaction they've been looking for all along. This is why Paul wrote, "We...are fellow workers for your joy; for by faith you stand" (2 Corinthians 1:24). It's the greatest win-win situation ever known to man. As God is most stunningly reflected in our lives, we're most profoundly satisfied in our souls.

More Than Morality

When a person truly honors God, something about his or her life reflects and exudes the presence of God Himself, not just the absence of wrong.

New Covenant spirituality calls us to far more than morality. It beckons us to *godliness,* a kind of living that's God-scented through and through. We can think of morality as the absence of anything wrong. But that's only the beginning. Godliness is the radiant, unmistakable presence of what is good, supernaturally good. It's a Spirit-led, Spirit-dependent, Spirit-produced kind of goodness.

Lewis Sperry Chafer describes true spirituality as "a divine output of the life, rather than a mere cessation of things which are called 'worldly.' True spirituality does not consist in what one does *not* do, it is rather what one *does*. It is not suppression: it is expression. It is not holding in self: it is living out Christ."[1]

Mere morality is a garden where the weeds have been pulled, but nothing has taken their place. It's a bare plot of land, containing nothing wrong, but exhibiting nothing that catches the eye. Godliness is a garden where the weeds have been pulled *and* the flora of heaven (see Galatians 5:22-23) is clearly blooming.

In Ephesians 4, Paul urges us beyond morality to the higher plane of godliness. He takes everyday situations and tells us to infuse them with supernatural responses, responses that have an unmistakable element of surprise in them.

He tells us to put away lying, but to go beyond just the absence of falsehood: "'Let each one of you speak truth with his neighbor,' for we are members of one another" (Ephesians 4:25). That's what it takes for something of the presence of God to be felt. It isn't enough to stop lying, nor is it enough to just keep quiet. There must be movement into life that's reflective of our Lord—like Him, we're to proclaim what is true.

The one who used to steal is to "steal no longer," Paul said (4:28). Yet this also isn't enough in itself. The former thief is now to "labor, working with his hands what is good, that he may have something to give him who has need" (4:28). The same hands that once took *from* the pockets of others are now to work honorably and put money *into* the pockets of those in need. In that way we reflect the integrity and compassion of our Lord through His indwelling Spirit.

We're to let no "corrupt word" (speech that tears down others) come from our lips—and then go beyond that to use our mouth for "what is good for necessary edification, that it may impart grace to the hearers" (4:29). It isn't enough that our speech doesn't destroy others; it must also positively build them into greater Christlikeness.

We're to put away relationally destructive things like "bitterness, wrath, anger, clamor…evil speaking…all malice" (4:31), then move beyond that to proactively "be kind to one another, tenderhearted, forgiving one another, even as God in Christ forgave you" (4:32).

We're not only to refrain from the wrong; we're also to reflect the supernaturally right.

This is where the element of surprise becomes so crucial. When our highest goal is to keep our noses clean, when our spiritual agenda consists in keeping ourselves back from sin, about the best thing that can happen is that people become impressed with our integrity and uprightness. But the reality is that we've done only what good Muslims, Jews, and even atheists do every day.

Erwin Lutzer writes about a portion of Chicago that has 160,000 quite distinguished inhabitants:

> None drinks a drop of liquor: not a one smokes; not a one dances; not a one goes to the movies. I mentioned that to a friend, and he said he would really like to visit this section of the city, maybe even move there. I told him that someday that might actually be possible. The area of the city, however, is Rose Hill Cemetery! You see, some who define the Christian life by what they don't do just miss the point.[2]

What a great illustration of the limitations of mere morality!

To genuinely glorify God requires walking the extra mile beyond morality. If a Roman soldier compelled a Jew to carry his backpack for one mile, then one mile was all he needed to go. No rabbi would have commanded anything more. But what Jesus told His followers in essence was this: "There'll be no surprise factor in your life if you only go one mile. God has placed you on this earth for something far grander than just responsible living and dutifully doing what you're commanded. He stationed you here to know Him intimately and to be His living, breathing marketing agency. And if you do only what's required, you won't get anyone's attention. Even worse, their attention will stop at you.

"So instead, without complaining, take that soldier's backpack and walk a full extra mile before you give it back to him. Is that fair? Of course not. But none of us is here to be treated fairly. We're here to draw attention to the God who drips with the most unfair thing in the universe—grace. This is the grace you'll show that soldier by walking the extra mile, a grace that will cause him to at least ponder why you would do that. Through his pondering you may have the chance to tell him about Me, the God so unlike his gods. For which of his gods ever compelled a man to walk an extra mile with his backpack?"

MAKING GOD VISIBLE

William Gladstone was prime minister of England and a devout Christian. As he walked home from work each day, he would sometimes pick out a young boy or two off the street and invite them home with him for dinner. Mrs. Gladstone never knew who to expect for dinner when he came home!

At one juncture of his career, he gave a speech to the House of Commons in which he quoted many statistics prepared for him by a high-ranking government statistician. As it turned out, the newspapers did their own research and discovered many of the figures to be badly erroneous. Gladstone was crucified in the London papers for the figures he gave out.

After all this had made the press, the statistician was summoned to Gladstone's office. He went fully expecting to be rebuked and fired, and rightfully so. When he was seated, Gladstone said to him, "I know how much you must be disturbed over what has happened and I have sent for you to put you at your ease. For a long time you have been engaged in handling the intricacies of the national accounts and this is the first mistake that you have made. I want to congratulate you and express to you my keen appreciation." With that he warmly shook the man's hand and let him go back to work.

My guess is that the man shook his head in astonishment all the way back. It's this surprise factor that preaches louder than any sermon we can deliver.

What would this look like practically today? Let me give you a few examples from people in our congregation:

- A lawyer in a large firm not only treats his staff fairly, but takes the
  time and trouble to learn the names of the many, many interns and

part-time staff in his firm. They're so surprised and pleased that he knows their names that he has been able to have significant ministry into many of their lives.

- A restaurant owner gives exceptionally high bonuses to his employees each Christmas, regardless of what his profits have been that year.
- A coach not only doesn't use profanity but invites the kids on his team over to his house and treats them like members of his family. He's been a surrogate father to countless young men who have no father at home.
- A family consistently brings in unwed expectant mothers to live with them during the pregnancy. They stay in close touch afterward and continue supporting the mothers however they can. Many of these girls have come to know Christ.
- A doctor joyously gives countless free hours to the poor and to people in the church in special need.

These are just a few examples of what I mean about moving past morality to godliness. Each of them would tell you the reason behind the kind of things they do is the God who indwells them.

When we talk about beckoning others to a more God-honoring plane of living, we must be sure that we're inviting them to nothing short of a lifestyle that requires God. It's utterly Spirit-dependent from beginning to end, and anything less is a quenching of the Spirit no matter how respectable it may appear. The bottom line is this: New Covenant application makes God more patently visible on the playing field of life.

MORE PERSONAL SATISFACTION

We supernaturally influence others by beckoning them not only to a more God-honoring life but also to a more *personally satisfying* plane of living. And these two realities are inseparable.

One of the wondrous realities of the New Covenant is that God has made His glory and our satisfaction to be synchronized with each other. Our longing for personal satisfaction and God's resolve for personal glorification are not opposed to each other, as is so often supposed. We'll find ourselves most deeply satisfied and invigorated when we're most dominated and intoxicated by God and His glory. It's absolutely a win-win situation. When we beckon believers to a more God-honoring way of life, we're really inviting them to do themselves the greatest favor they possibly can.

Jonathan Edwards writes, "God in seeking his glory, seeks the good of his creatures...God is their good."[3] John Piper writes in this same regard, "Thus the exhibition of God's glory and the deepest joy of human souls are one thing. The implications of this are breathtaking."[4]

We find this alluded to, among many places, in the Upper Room Discourse. It's the great reward for genuine obedience. "He who has My commandments and keeps them, it is he who loves Me. And he who loves Me will be loved by My Father, and I will love him and manifest [make known] Myself to him" (John 14:21). "If anyone loves Me, he will keep My word; and My Father will love him, and We will come to him and make Our home with him" (14:23). Christ promises two great rewards here for obedience to His Word.

First, genuine obedience brings a superlative, experiential sense of God's love. These verses don't mean that God loves the obedient believer more than the disobedient one, but they do clearly show that the obedient one is more experientially in touch with this great love.

When we beckon others to a more God-honoring way of life, we're also inviting them to have their hearts ravished in new ways by Christ's love. We need make no apologies for the price that must be paid in order for this to happen. Certainly Christ didn't.

Second, obedience brings a more intimate knowledge of Christ and the Father. "We will come to him and make Our home with him" (John

14:23) is the alluring promise of special, personal familiarity with the Son and the Father. Yet this kind of privileged intimacy bears a price tag— obedient responsiveness to the commands of Christ. Is it worth the cost? Only those who have tasted such intimacy know that all things are as dung in comparison (see Philippians 3:8).

This is wrapped up beautifully in the words of our Lord in John 15:1-11, the great passage on abiding. He gives us the ultimate purpose for our abiding: "By this My Father is glorified, that you bear much fruit; so you will be My disciples" (15:8). As we bear much God-produced fruit, the Father's glory is made known on earth. This never happens by our going out and trying to bear fruit; it happens only as we significantly abide in Christ. The inevitable by-product of that abiding will be luxuriant fruit bearing. "I am the vine, you are the branches. He who abides in Me, and I in him, bears much fruit; for without Me you can do nothing" (15:5).

What about us? If we spend our days for the purpose of much fruit bearing, then God gets great glory; but is there anything in it for us? Ah, yes, my friend, in spades. Listen to the words of Jesus: "These things I have spoken to you, that My joy may remain in you, and that your joy may be full" (15:11). Do we want fullness of joy? Of course. The only way to get it is to have the Son of God's joy supernaturally dwelling within. And the only way to get that is abiding in this same Son of God.

Oceans of Joy

What is joy? One person called it "the echo of God's life within." C. S. Lewis made an important distinction in separating joy from happiness or pleasure. Happiness comes as a result of favorable external circumstances. Pleasure comes as the result of having a bodily appetite fulfilled. Both are legitimate and have an appropriate place in the Christian's life.

But joy is different from these two. It's wholly independent of external circumstances or bodily enjoyment. It's the indescribable enjoyment of the living, breathing presence of God. "In Your presence is fullness of joy; at Your right hand are pleasures forevermore" (Psalm 16:11). I call it indescribable because it's a kind of happiness that defies explaining to someone who has never tasted it. But it's also a kind of happiness that outstrips happiness or pleasure. Kirby Page writes, "The word 'joy' is too great and grand to be confused with the superficial things we call 'happiness.' It was joy and peace that Jesus said He left men in His will." How then is this "joy" different from "happiness"?

It's first of all a *cleaner* happiness than either of these. It possesses an untainted purity that comes from its source—the One in whom there is no darkness whatsoever (see 1 John 1:5).

It's also a *stronger* happiness than either of the others, a vibrancy that others can't match. "You have put gladness in my heart, more than in the season that their grain and wine increased" (Psalm 4:7).

And it's a *deeper* happiness than the others. This joy springs from the deepest part of our being. "Out of his heart [or "innermost being"] will flow rivers of living water" (John 7:38). I remember thinking soon after I became a Christian that here was a happiness that went deeper into me than anything I'd ever known before. I now know that I was tasting joy for the first time.

I'm convinced that many of God's children think they're experiencing joy when it's really just happiness or pleasure. I'm also convinced that there are oceans of joy that we all have yet to taste; in fact eternity will be spent doing just that.

In the meantime, we have the joy and privilege of beckoning and inviting others to this win-win situation. The depths of our souls are most fully thrilled as God is most fully delighted in and reflected through our earthly lives. J. Campbell White of the Layman's Missionary Movement wrote these words:

Nothing can wholly satisfy the life of Christ within His followers except the adoption of Christ's purpose for the world He came to redeem. Fame, pleasure and riches are but husks and ashes in contrast with the boundless and abiding joy of working with God for the fulfillment of His eternal plans.[5]

Indeed, no greater joy or adventure exists on earth than working with God to advance His purposes in others' hearts. To see unbelievers come to Christ and believers grow in maturity diffuses a joy throughout our inner self found nowhere else. It's the high adventure of white-water Christianity. It's the vibrant rest of supernatural influencing. It's the releasing of the rivers within. It's what we were made for.

A Golden Eagle—and His Leap of Faith

> I'd rather be ashes than dust. I'd rather my spark
> go out in a burning flame than to be stifled
> with dry rot. I'd rather be a splendid meteor blazing
> across the sky, every atom in me a magnificent glow,
> than to be a sleepy and permanent planet.
> Life is meant to be lived, not just to exist.
>
> JACK LONDON

I've often told the first part of the following story. Then some friends of mine, Thomas Womack and Doug Gabbert, after hearing it from me, developed the parable even further. In many ways they've captured the heartbeat of what I'm trying to say in this book. Perhaps you can identify with this longer version as strongly as I do.

A FLEETING SHADOW

A story is told about a Native American boy who happened upon a nest of golden eagle eggs in the mountains. Deciding to have some fun, the boy took one of the eggs, carried it with him down from the mountains, and placed it in the nest of some prairie chickens.

The egg hatched, and the newborn bird grew up with the brood of prairie chickens. Believing himself to be like everyone else around him, he behaved accordingly. He clucked and cackled and scratched in the dirt for seeds and insects to live on. He never tried flying more than several inches off the ground, since prairie chickens are incapable of rising much higher.

Months went by. One day the young eagle was scratching along with one of his older prairie chicken brothers when a fleeting shadow passed over them. He looked up and saw, high in the sky, the soaring form of something gliding on the currents of the wind.

"What a beautiful bird!" he exclaimed.

"That's an eagle," the older brother informed him, staring upward. "A golden eagle. He's the king of the air. No bird can compare with him." Then he lowered his gaze and added, "But don't give it a second thought…you could never be like him."

So the younger brother tried to give it no more thought, but somehow he couldn't erase from his mind the image of that eagle soaring up there near the clouds.

ANOTHER SHADOW

It wasn't long before he was growing quite a bit larger than his prairie chicken brothers and sisters. In fact, they started calling him Clunk because his body was so big and awkward as he plodded along on his over-sized feet, and as he bent his bulky frame to scratch in the dirt for bugs with everyone else.

One early morning he was especially irritated by the way the others were mocking him all the time, and he allowed himself to wander off some distance to be away from them for a while. Slowly he made his way toward the rising slope of a nearby ridge. His neck and shoulders were sore and achy from constantly bending over, but as usual he was ravenously hungry, so he continued bobbing his head close to the ground to scratch and root for some breakfast. All those ants and acorns and slugs and grubs and beetles and roaches—there sure wasn't much taste to any of it, but what else was there to eat? In fact, what else was there to life at all besides scratching around like this in the dirt? He wished he knew.

Suddenly, he noticed a shadow passing over him again, and he was reminded of that day when the eagle had flown so high overhead. But this time the shadow didn't pass on.

Clunk slowly raised his head from the ground. Standing there before him he saw a towering majestic bird with piercing eyes. The sunlight shimmered on the golden feathers of his head so that he seemed almost to be wearing a crown.

A shiver of fear shot through Clunk's achy neck and shoulders. He forced himself to speak. "Who…are you?"

"My name is Avian," his visitor replied in a voice that was deep and strong. "If you want to find out what your life is truly meant to be, then follow me…and don't look back." Avian turned around and quickly began stepping up the rough slope of the ridge.

Clunk had to make a decision fast. Something inside told him to get back to scratching in the dirt as usual. But something deeper inside told him to hurry and catch up with this Avian, whoever he was. And that's what Clunk did.

The Impossible Climb

The minutes turned to hours as they continued upward, step by step, and the slope turned into a steep and rocky mountainside. Avian kept a strong and steady pace, and now and then he even whistled as he walked, but he often turned to look over his shoulder at his companion.

It took all of Clunk's strength and energy to keep up. He was short of breath, his feathers were soaked with sweat, and his legs were burning with pain. More and more he was thinking what a horrible mistake he'd made.

Why hadn't he realized before what a good life he had down there below? While scratching in the dirt for food wasn't particularly tasty or exciting, at least it was easy and natural and comfortable. He seriously considered turning around immediately and dropping to lower ground again to rejoin his fellow prairie chickens.

But every time Clunk stopped to turn back, Avian would look over his shoulder at him with those piercing eyes and with the sun's rays gleaming on his head. Clunk found himself afraid to do anything except stagger onward. He kept following along, gazing ahead with amazement at Avian's boundless and happy strength.

At one point, Clunk managed to get enough breath to ask, "Where are we going?"

"On high," Avian answered.

But the way grew rockier and steeper than ever. Clunk tried his hardest to match every step that Avian took, but it was just too much. Finally Clunk collapsed, falling down against the stones.

Avian came and stood over him. "Do you want to keep going?"

Clunk was gasping for breath. "Is...is it much farther?"

"Yes. We have far to go. We're not yet even halfway up."

Clunk groaned. "Then...then it really doesn't matter what I want, does it? I can't make it anyway. I know I can't."

"Yes," Avian replied, "what you want *does* matter. Do you wish to keep going?"

Clunk couldn't understand. What a nightmare he'd gotten himself into! But something inside him was longing to go onward. Something inside told him that he never wanted to scratch in the dirt again, that there had to be a better life. Something deep within told him that he actually wanted to be...like Avian.

"Yes," Clunk answered. "Yes...I want to keep going."

He forced himself up from the rocks and tried standing, but his legs crumpled beneath him. He tried once more but fell again.

In frustration and despair, he sighed and closed his eyes; then he felt something warm closing around him. Avian was wrapping his wings under him and lifting him up and stepping onward. He was carrying him up the mountain!

More hours went by. At first, Clunk was too worn out to notice how much effort this was costing Avian. But in time he became aware of Avian's panting breath and heaving chest and the fact that he didn't whistle anymore. The look in Avian's eyes was still determined and focused, but Clunk could see weariness there as well.

Their pace was no longer quick and steady, but slow and arduous. Every step was a struggle. Clunk could see lines of pain on Avian's brow.

"Perhaps I should try walking on my own again," Clunk said. "You can let me down if you want."

"No," said Avian. "This is the only way that you'll make it to where we're going."

THE SUMMIT REACHED

So they continued. The afternoon shadows lengthened, but step by grueling step they went onward, clambering over boulders and crags. The sun sank behind them and the daylight faded, but even in the deepening night they kept going.

Avian never rested, though his every breath seemed to be an ordeal. He held Clunk close in his wings, and Clunk could feel the rapid pounding of Avian's heart. It was beating so swiftly that Clunk truly feared for Avian's life. But still they kept climbing, through the blackest hours of the night. Clunk sometimes fell into a fitful sleep, but each time he awoke in the darkness, he could hear Avian's struggling breaths and feel Avian's racing heartbeat. And each time, he sensed Avian's wings wrapped around him more securely than ever.

The first glimmer of dawn finally appeared in the sky. Clunk was afraid to ask Avian anything; he was sure Avian would have neither the strength nor the breath to answer him. But suddenly Avian spoke up: "We're nearly there." His voice was weak and strained.

His final steps seemed to be the slowest and most agonizing of all. And then, just as the circle of the sun began rising, they reached the summit. Struggling for breath, Avian gently laid Clunk down on the smooth stone ledge at the mountain's very peak.

"It's finished," Avian said. "We're here."

Clunk looked out at the vista stretching before them. Far below he could see forested ridges and velvet-green meadows and twisting canyons with rivers that roared. Farther out on the horizon was the vast blue mirror of the ocean.

He'd never seen anything like this. For a long, silent moment, he stared at the view, trying to take it all in.

To the Wind

Finally he turned to Avian. The rich red light of sunrise made his golden feathers shine more splendidly than ever; his face was etched with exhaustion, and yet Avian was smiling at him.

"Avian...this is so beautiful. But I don't understand. What happens now?"

Toward the horizon, Avian arched out one of his wings to its full extension. Clunk was amazed at how long it was.

"Everything you see," Avian said, "everything out there—it's all yours to enjoy."

"But how would I ever get down there?"

"By soaring."

"Oh, please don't joke with me, Avian. Tell me the truth. Am I stuck up here? It would take me weeks to scramble down off this peak by myself.

You need to know something: I'm so stumbly and clumsy that everyone at home calls me Clunk."

"No," Avian replied sternly, "that's not your name. Your true name is Windsor. You were made to soar; you're *meant* to soar. I'm rested now, and I'll show you how."

"You mean *you* can fly?"

"I can…and you've already seen it. One day my shadow passed right over you while you were pecking for bugs."

"But then why did you stagger all day and night up this mountain like that? Why didn't you just fly up?"

"If I had," replied Avian, "would you have followed me here?"

"Of course not."

"Then there's your answer. Now then, watch me." Avian cocked his wings and took a quick graceful leap into the air.

In fear, Clunk almost reached out to try and stop him. But he was glad he didn't. He'd never seen anything more thrilling than the sight of Avian wheeling and gliding and lofting on the air currents. It brought tears to Clunk's eyes to see it, and an unexplainable aching in his heart.

After a few moments, Avian swooped in toward the stone ledge. His landing brought a rush of air that ruffled Clunk's feathers.

"Now, Windsor, it's your turn," Avian said.

"Oh no."

"Oh yes. You're an eagle, Windsor, and nothing less. You're a golden eagle, just like me. In fact, you're my younger brother. And it's time to live like it."

"What?"

"Just spread your wings, then leap out."

"Just— Oh, but—"

"Trust me, Windsor. You already have everything it takes. Everything you need."

"But—"

"I'll go first, then you follow me."

"But—"

"Windsor, to get you up here, I gave it everything I had. Now I want you to believe me and listen and do exactly what I say. Then give it everything *you* have."

"But—"

"Don't think about it. Just launch out, and don't look back."

"No! Wait—"

"No, Windsor, there's no need to wait any longer." With that, Avian launched out again, leaving behind another gust of air that ruffled Clunk's feathers. From out in the sky Avian at once called back over his shoulder, "Now, Windsor! *Now!*"

Without thinking, Windsor spread his wings…and leaped…and never looked back.

Now he understood so clearly, for the first time, why he'd never been fulfilled by prairie chicken living. He was an eagle, created to soar on high and to know the deep thrill that only golden eagle living can bring. His heart could be satisfied by nothing less…even though soaring could be frightening at times.

Nor can *your* life be satisfied with anything less. Go ahead…take the jump!

It's what you were made for.

A Tighter Grip

Reality and vision are very often not the same things. A vision of how things could be (or should be), and an honest appraisal of how things actually are is very often a humbling affair.

This most certainly holds true in the book you've just read. As I said at the outset, I've sought to lay out a vision for helping you influence others in a way that is supernatural, not just natural—an approach to life and ministry that absolutely requires God to pull it off. In laying this out before you, I trust you're under no illusion that I've fully mastered the things I've written. As I said in the introduction, this book is an invitation to join me in a journey that I'm very imperfectly taking myself.

While I believe that I've tasted God's power in and through my life in some important ways, those tastes are by no means as frequent as I would wish for. On a daily basis my personal reality falls short of the biblical vision—many times far short.

Just today I've been curt with my sons, neglectful of my wife, and jealous of another's success. I've dropped names and battled powerful lustful urges. And this is Sunday—the day we ministers are supposed to be at our best! And the day's not close to being over yet. How scary is that?

In many ways this book has been painful to write, every chapter requiring confession and varying levels of repentance. At times I've been tempted to give it up. Yet through it all, a beam of light has compelled me to keep moving forward, however imperfectly and inconsistently. That beam of light is the simple thought that *God has a far tighter grip on me than I have on Him.*

Therein lies my great hope—and yours. The God who created us, who secured our salvation at the cost of His only Son's blood, is the same God who actually resides within us, who refuses to be put off by our failures, who will never give up on our growth, who sees hope in our lives where we see none.

The sole hope any of us has is that where there is nothing but desert, out of the barren wasteland of our natural being, God—God alone—can bring forth streams of living water. Whatever sins you've committed, however worthless you may think yourself to be, however dysfunctional the home you grew up in, the currents of God's Spirit are still pressing forward in your life. Nothing is strong enough to hold back the tide of God.

These divine currents keep us from being satisfied with sin or spiritual complacency. They urge us forward to fuller abandonment, and they refresh our hope that maybe, just maybe, God can still do something big through our lives.

Indeed He can. And indeed He will, though many times we can't see it. Our journey forward will, in fact, be hampered at times by our own failure, unbelief, and pride. But don't let Satan do to you what I too often allow him to do to me—get me so focused on failures and sin that I lose sight of the grip God has on me. Whatever else our rebellion and shortcomings may do, they cannot shake us free from God's tight hold on our lives.

We're inscribed on the palms of His hands (see Isaiah 49:16). And those hands—universe-producing, nail-pierced, scepter-wielding, life-orchestrating hands—have us in their grip, a grip that's infinitely tighter on us than our hold on Him.

That's our reason never to give up: hands mighty enough to toss the galaxies into existence, loving enough to endure the burning agony of man's hatred, righteous enough to rule the everlasting kingdom of God, and skilled enough to handle all the intricate details of my life and yours.

God's grip is infinitely tighter on us than ours is on Him. I hope you never recover from this truth. And because of this—though our journey into the land of supernatural influencing will often be checkered by failure, hampered by unbelief, and temporarily stalled by pride—God will never, ever bail on us. Like a father teaching his child how to ride a bike, He will not view any failure as final or any spill as permanent. He dusts us off, helps us back on the bike, and leads us back on the road.

His Spirit will continue moving, prodding, convicting, and encouraging us into the white water of His river flow. It's what we're made for, and He won't allow us to be satisfied with anything less. God is too passionate for His own glory and too concerned for our own good to leave us alone in the desert. He'll pull out all the stops to move us to that place we most belong—releasing the rivers within!

Notes

Introduction

1. John Stott, as quoted by J. Oswald Sanders, *Shoe-Leather Commitment* (Chicago: Moody, 1990), 83.
2. Oswald Chambers, *Biblical Ethics* (CD-ROM, United Kingdom: Marshall Morgan & Scott, 1947).
3. George Grella, "James Bond: Culture Hero," *The New Republic,* May 1964, 17-20.

Chapter 1

1. A. W. Tozer, *The Pursuit of God* (Camp Hill, Pa.: Christian Publications, 1993), 11.
2. Martin Luther, *Commentary on Galatians,* ed. John Prince Fallowes (Grand Rapids, Mich.: Kregel, 1979), 238.
3. Oswald Chambers, *My Utmost for His Highest* (CD-ROM, United Kingdom: Marshall Morgan & Scott, 1927).
4. Oswald Chambers, *Disciples Indeed* (CD-ROM, United Kingdom: Marshall Morgan & Scott, 1955).
5. Max Lucado, *A Love Worth Giving* (Nashville: W, 2002), 82.
6. Frederick W. Faber, as quoted by A. W. Tozer, *The Knowledge of the Holy* (New York: HarperCollins, 1961), 16.
7. Dr. Martyn Lloyd-Jones, *Joy Unspeakable* (Colorado Springs, Colo.: Shaw, 1984), 18.
8. Bruce Barton, "There Are Two Seas," *McCall's,* 1928.

CHAPTER 2

1. George Müller, as quoted by John Piper, *Desiring God* (Portland, Oreg.: Multnomah, 1986), 116.

2. Samuel Rutherford, as quoted by J. Oswald Sanders, *Shoe-Leather Commitment* (Chicago: Moody, 1990), 25.

3. Jonathan Edwards, as quoted by John Piper, *God's Passion for His Glory* (Wheaton Ill.: Crossway, 1998), 33.

4. Henry Scougal, *The Life of God in the Soul of Man* (Scotland: Christian Focus, 2001), 109.

5. C. S. Lewis, *The Weight of Glory* (New York: Macmillan, 1980), 3.

6. A. W. Tozer, *The Pursuit of God* (Camp Hill, Pa.: Christian Publications, 1982), 42.

7. John Piper, *God's Passion for His Glory* (Wheaton, Ill.: Crossway, 1998), 81.

8. J. Oswald Sanders, *Spiritual Lessons* (Chicago: Moody, 1971), 184.

9. George MacDonald, *George MacDonald: An Anthology,* ed. C. S. Lewis (New York: Touchstone, 1996), 58.

10. John Stott, *Evangelism: Why and How* (Downers Grove, Ill.: InterVarsity, 1962), 29.

11. Dr. Robert Munger: as quoted in "Quotations on Evangelism," *Entplaza,* 16 April 2003, found at www.entplaza.com/cgi-bin/create/quotes.pl?cat=Evangelism.

12. C. S. Lewis, as quoted by John Piper, *God's Passion for His Glory* (Wheaton, Ill.: Crossway, 1998), 46.

13. A. W. Tozer, *Signposts: A Collection of Sayings from A. W. Tozer,* comp. Harry Verploegh (Wheaton, Ill.: Victor, 1988), 111.

14. John Piper, *The Supremacy of God in Preaching* (Grand Rapids, Mich.: Baker, 1990), 24.
15. Henry Martyn, as quoted by John Sargent, *Life and Letters of Henry Martyn* (Carlisle, Pa.: Banner of Truth Trust, 1985).

CHAPTER 3

1. Samuel Brengle, as quoted by J. Oswald Sanders, *Spiritual Leadership* (Chicago: Moody, 1980), 90.
2. J. Oswald Sanders, *Spiritual Leadership* (Chicago: Moody, 1980), 35.
3. J. Oswald Sanders, *Spiritual Leadership* (Chicago: Moody, 1980), 33.
4. J. Oswald Sanders, *Enjoying Intimacy With God* (Chicago: Moody, 1980).
5. W. Garden Blaikie, *The Personal Life of David Livingstone* (New York: Negro Universities Press, 1969), 442.
6. Beatrice Clelland, "Portrait of a Christian," *Priscilla's Friends,* 16 April 2003, www.priscillasfriends.org/studies/water.html.

CHAPTER 4

1. C. S. Lewis, *Mere Christianity* (New York: HarperCollins, 2001), 199.
2. Dorothy L. Sayers, "Creed or Chaos?" *The Whimsical Christian* (New York: Macmillan, 1978), 34-5.
3. G. Walter Hansen, "The Emotions of Jesus," *Christianity Today,* 27 February 1997, 42.
4. A. W. Tozer, *The Root of the Righteous* (Harrisburg, Pa.: Christian Publications, 1955), 8.

5. Augustine, as quoted by Bruce Shelley, *All the Saints Adore Thee* (Grand Rapids, Mich.: Zondervan, 1988), 40.

6. Jonathan Edwards, *The Works of Jonathan Edwards,* vol. 2 (Carlisle, Pa.: The Banner of Truth Trust, 1986), 14.

7. Frederick W. Faber, as quoted by A. W. Tozer, *The Pursuit of God* (Camp Hill, Pa.: Christian Publications, 1993), 38-9.

8. Jonathan Edwards, *Religious Affections* (Portland, Oreg.: Multnomah, 1984), 26.

9. H. C. G. Moule, *Colossians and Philemon Studies* (Grand Rapids, Mich.: Zondervan, 2002), 55.

10. A. J. Gordon, as quoted by E. M. Bounds, *The Complete Works of E. M. Bounds on Prayer* (Grand Rapids, Mich.: Baker, 1990), 432.

11. George MacLeod, as quoted by Edythe Draper, *Draper's Book of Quotations for the Christian World* (Wheaton, Ill.: Tyndale, 1992).

12. Henry Martyn, as quoted by John Sargent, *Life and Letters of Henry Martyn* (Carlisle, Pa.: Banner of Truth Trust, 1985).

CHAPTER 5

1. Joe Aldrich, *Lifestyle Evangelism* (Sisters, Oreg.: Multnomah, 1993), 95.

2. Erwin Lutzer, *Who Are You to Judge?* (Chicago: Moody, 2002), 218.

3. Joe Aldrich, *Lifestyle Evangelism* (Sisters, Oreg.: Multnomah, 1993), 44.

CHAPTER 6

1. J. Wilbur Chapman, as quoted by J. Oswald Sanders, *Spiritual Lessons* (Chicago: Moody, 1971), 188.

2. Oswald Chambers, *My Utmost for His Highest* (CD-ROM, United Kingdom: Marshall Morgan & Scott, 1927).

3. Phillips Brooks, *Sermons* (New York: E. P. Dutton, 1879), 340.

4. Larry Crabb, "New Way Living," message given at Grace Bible Church, College Station, Texas, 8 April 2001.

5. John Calvin, *Commentaries,* ed. David W. Torrance and Thomas F. Torrance, trans. A.W. Morrison (Grand Rapids, Mich.: Eerdmans, 1972), 245.

6. Martin Luther, as quoted by "Weekly Quotes," *Christ the King Presbyterian Church,* 21 December 2000, found at www.ctkpca.org.

7. A. W. Tozer, as quoted by J. Oswald Sanders, *Spiritual Leadership* (Chicago: Moody, 1980), 35.

8. Nancy Leigh DeMoss, *Brokenness: The Heart God Revives* (Chicago: Moody, 2002), 125.

9. Jonathan Edwards, "Sermon 1: God Glorified in Man's Dependence," *The Works of Jonathan Edwards* (Carlisle, Pa.: The Banner of Truth Trust, 1986), 3.

10. C. S. Lewis, *The Quotable Lewis,* ed. Wayne Martindale and Jerry Root (Wheaton, Ill.: Tyndale, 1989), 156.

11. John Wesley, *The Works of John Wesley* (Grand Rapids, Mich.: Zondervan, 1959), 437.

12. Samuel Chadwick, as quoted by George Verwer, *Come, Live, Die* (Wheaton, Ill.: Tyndale, 1972), 83.

13. Henry Ward Beecher, *Life of Jesus the Christ (The Works of Henry Ward Beecher: 1813–1887),* 25 April 2003, found at www. geocities.com/snoopythewriter/BEECHER.html.

CHAPTER 7

1. C. S. Lewis, *The Quotable Lewis,* ed. Wayne Martindale and Jerry Root (Wheaton, Ill.: Tyndale, 1989), 351.

2. David Livingstone, as quoted by John Piper, *Desiring God* (Portland, Oreg.: Multnomah, 1986), 201-2.

CHAPTER 8

1. No author given, *Biblical Studies Foundation,* 2000, 16 April 2003, found at www.bible.org/docs/splife/know/know-05.htm.
2. Max Lucado, *A Love Worth Giving* (Nashville: W, 2002), 163.
3. Dinah Maria Craik, *A Life for a Life,* 1859, *Literary Heritage,* 4 April 2003, found at www3.shropshire-cc.gov.uk/intros /T000165.htm.
4. John Greenleaf Whittier, "Miriam," *Complete Poetical Works of John Greenleaf Whittier,* ed. Horace E. Scudder (Boston: Houghton Mifflin, 1892), 95.
5. Martin Luther, as quoted by John Stott, *I Believe in Preaching* (London: Hodder and Stoughton, 1982), 25.
6. Joshua Swartz, as quoted by Dwight Edwards, "Philippians: Earthly Conduct of Heavenly Citizens," *Biblical Studies Foundation,* 2000, 16 April 2003, found at www.bible.org/docs /nt/books/phi/phil-d.htm.
7. C. S. Lewis in a letter to Sheldon Vanauken on 22 April 1953, as quoted by Sheldon Vanauken, *A Severe Mercy* (San Francisco: Harper and Row, 1977), 134.
8. Alexander Maclaren, as quoted by *Closer Walk New Testament,* ed. Bruce H. Wilkinson (Grand Rapids, Mich.: Zondervan, 1990), 409.

CHAPTER 9

1. Charles Finney, as quoted by J. Oswald Sanders, *Bible Men of Faith* (Chicago: Moody, 1965), 145.

2. Robert Lowry, *The Hymnal for Worship & Celebration* (Waco, Tex.: Word Music, 1976), 195.

CHAPTER 10

1. A. W. Tozer, *Signposts: A Collection of Sayings from A. W. Tozer,* comp. Harry Verploegh (Wheaton, Ill.: Victor, 1988), 185.
2. John Eldredge, from *Preaching Today Audio,* found at http://christianitytoday.aol.com/ct/2000/003/33.86.html.
3. Clarence E. Macartney, *Macartney's Illustrations* (Nashville, Tenn.: Abingdon, 1946), 136.

CHAPTER 11

1. Lewis Sperry Chafer, *He That is Spiritual* (Grand Rapids, Mich.: Zondervan, 1967), 60.
2. Erwin Lutzer, *Who Are You to Judge?* (Chicago: Moody, 2002), 219.
3. Jonathan Edwards, as quoted by John Piper, *God's Passion for His Glory* (Wheaton, Ill.: Crossway, 1998), 32-3.
4. John Piper, *God's Passion for His Glory* (Wheaton, Ill.: Crossway, 1998), 33.
5. J. Campbell White, as quoted by John Piper, *Desiring God* (Portland, Oreg.: Multnomah, 1986), 186.